THE EVANGELISTIC LOVE OF GOD AND NEIGHBOR

THE EVANGELISTIC LOVE OF GOD & NEIGHBOR

A THEOLOGY OF WITNESS AND DISCIPLESHIP

SCOTT J. JONES

Abingdon Press
Nashville

THE EVANGELISTIC LOVE OF GOD AND NEIGHBOR
A THEOLOGY OF WITNESS AND DISCIPLESHIP

Copyright © 2003 by Abingdon Press

This book is printed on acid-free paper.

Library of Congress Cataloging-in-Publication Data

Jones, Scott J. The evangelistic love of God and neighbor : a theology of witness and
    discipleship / Scott J. Jones.
        p. cm.
Includes bibliographical references and index.
    ISBN 0-687-04614-9 (adhesive : alk. paper)
    1. Evangelistic work. 2. Witness bearing (Christianity). 3. United Methodist Church (U.S).—
Doctrines. I. Title.

    BV3790.J665
    2003 269'.2—dc22

                                                                            2003015833

ISBN 13: 978-0-687-04614-0

All scripture quotations, unless otherwise noted, are from the *New Revised Standard Version of the
Bible,* copyright © 1989, Division of Christian Education of the National Council of the Churches
of Christ in the United States of America. Used by permission. All rights reserved.

Scripture quotations noted (NIV) are taken from the HOLY BIBLE, NEW INTERNATIONAL VER-
SION®. NIV® Copyright © 1973, 1978, 1984 by International Bible Society. Used by permission of
Zondervan Publishing House. All rights reserved.

Scripture quotations noted (KJV) are from the King James or Authorized Version of the Bible.

The Graeca® font used to print this work is available from Linguist's Software, Inc., PO Box 580,
Edmonds, WA 98020-0580 tel (206) 775-1130.

07 08 09 10 11 12—10 9 8 7 6 5

MANUFACTURED IN THE UNITED STATES OF AMERICA

To Elizabeth Snell and Marty Cannaday, whose faith in Christ has been strong, whose passion for evangelism has been enduring, and whose determination to spend their lives in the Lord's work has been an inspiration to me and to my family. If this book helps to shape the ministry of future leaders in the church so that they love the Lord more fully and evangelize more effectively, Elizabeth and Marty will be pleased with my labors in this task. So may it be.

This book is also dedicated to the other members of First United Methodist Church, Howe, Texas, who taught me more about evangelism, faith, and prayer than I taught them during the four years I was their pastor. We learned much together, and I am grateful.

Freely to all ourselves we give,
Constrained by Jesu's love to live
    The servants of mankind.
Now, Jesu, now thy love impart,
To govern each devoted heart,
    And fit us for thy will!
Deep founded in the truth of grace,
Build up thy rising church, and place
    The city on the hill.
O let our faith and love abound!
O let our lives to all around
    With purest lustre shine!
That all around our works may see,
And give the glory, Lord, to thee,
    The heavenly light divine!

Charles Wesley
The Works of John Wesley,
Bicentennial Edition, 7:704

Contents

Part II   The Practice of Evangelism

Foreword

I hope this book accomplishes at least three purposes. First, I see it as a contribution to the field of evangelism that will help scholars, seminary students, and pastors think clearly about the definition, purposes, and practice of this important area of the church's ministry. I have sought to show a biblical foundation for it while articulating some possible connections to mission, discipleship, and witness.

Second, I hope this book advances the conversation among scholars in the field. I have intentionally referenced a number of works by other scholars to show how my position compares and contrasts with theirs. This ought to be standard in academic research. The work of one scholar should build on the work of others either by affirmation or rejection, with critical reflection and mutual respect. I noted in my article in the *Journal of the Academy for Evangelism in Theological Education*, however, a lack of such engagement.[1] Reviewing the literature in this field, I often found books and articles that did not take sufficient account of other significant studies. In that article I acknowledge that the academic study of evangelism is still a young discipline and is only now beginning to grow the academic infrastructure that it needs. It is my hope that this study will provoke deeper research on the many areas it addresses and spirited debate about its conclusions.

Third, I hope that the appendix of this book contributes to a conversation among pastors and church leaders about the practice of evangelism. It is one way of conceiving how the more abstract considerations of parts 1 and 2 might be put into practice in congregations. For those engaged in ministries of congregational evangelism, this approach may show a more concrete way forward to the improvement of the ministry in their contexts.

This book is the product of many years of ministry, including preaching, pastoring, teaching, reading, and thinking. It began in a class under David Lowes Watson at Perkins in 1980. It was nourished by three congregations (the United Methodist churches of Prosper, Howe, and Commerce, Texas) that I served as pastor. It was furthered through continuing dialogue with John Wesley and colleagues who seek to understand and interpret his thought for today. Students at Perkins School of Theology from 1997 to the present have helped me think through the issues. Colleagues who serve as professors of evangelism and who participate in the Academy for Evangelism in Theological Education have challenged me. Faculty colleagues at Perkins discussed my article "The Evangelistic Love of God and Neighbor" and helped me see a number of holes in its argument. Then at a crucial stage in my thinking a paper by Chris Harrison, one of my students, gave me the impetus to think more clearly about the ideas that now occupy chapters 3 and 4. I lectured on this topic at Cliff College in the United Kingdom, and the reactions by students there were helpful. I addressed many of these issues in the Hopkins Lectures at First United Methodist Church in Denton, Texas, and the Lenten Lecture Series at River Road United Methodist Church in Richmond, Virginia, and in many other workshops around the United States. The questions asked by clergy colleagues and laity alike have been stimulating.

I owe a great debt to William J. Abraham. For the last eighteen years we have been colleagues and arguing partners. As my teacher John Deschner once said of his relationship with Schubert Ogden, it is a blessing to have a theological friend. As will be evident from this volume, I am consciously building on what Abraham has done. At the same time, I think certain improvements and corrections are warranted, and I offer them in order to carry forward the work of the discipline we share. His previous writings on evangelism, our conversations over the years, and his careful reading of this manuscript have made me a better scholar.

In addition, Carole Walker, Greg Jones, Rebekah Miles, Ruben Habito, Jim Kirby, and Mary Lou Reece have read all or portions of this manuscript and made comments on it. Jason Vickers made many helpful editorial suggestions and Jacob Friesenhahn helped with research. I have benefited from their suggestions, but as always, the remaining mistakes are my responsibility.

As with my other books, I am indebted to my family. Their love, support, and constant encouragement for my writing projects has helped make this book possible. To Mary Lou, *sine qua, non.* To my children, Jameson, Arthur, and Marynell, I say thanks once again for believing in God and also in me.

Scott J. Jones
Dallas, Texas

The Theological Study
of Christian Evangelism

W hat is the gospel of Jesus Christ?[1] How is this gospel best shared with those who need it? I take these to be the two fundamental questions shaping the theological study of Christian evangelism. The first question, with all of its presuppositions and implications, involves the totality of systematic theology. It involves one's understanding of God, Christ, the Holy Spirit, the reign of God, the church, sin, salvation, justification, sanctification, and eschatology. Thus, a book about the theology of evangelism should begin with systematic theology.

This is one of the reasons that the subject of evangelism has been and continues to be so controversial within Christianity. When thinking about evangelism, one considers the content of the Christian faith. When practicing evangelism, one's theological commitments are clearly on display. The same relationship characterizes preaching, where one proclaims the gospel and should attend to all of its implications; to worship, where one names God and offers God appropriate praise and prayer; and to education, where one teaches the gospel to believers. In short, there is a relationship between systematic theology and practical theology.

Hence, this book will try to make clear the relationship between theology and the practice of evangelism.

The second question qualifies the first by inquiring about one way that Christians are called to live in response to the gospel. Some ways of construing the gospel may preclude the need to share it with anyone. Other ways may see the task of sharing the gospel with non-Christians as having such a low level of importance that the subject does not deserve much attention. Still others may find the question of deciding who is and who is not Christian to be so difficult that no responsible judgment is possible. In such a case, the prudent course would be not to share the gospel at all. Against these views I will argue that the church's ministry of sharing the gospel with non-Christians is a necessary and important corollary to the gospel message itself. Otherwise put, if Christianity does not have a strong evangelistic component, then it is inadequate.

The question about sharing the gospel also requires consideration of the persons being considered as recipients. Are we sharing it with nominal Christians living in a Christian culture? Secular persons who are post-Christian? Persons practicing other religions? Or are we simply helping practicing Christians to grow further in their discipleship? Some of the arguments about evangelism concern how best to identify the appropriate recipients of this ministry.

Many authors have cited the lack of an adequate definition of evangelism. David Barrett, for example, has chronicled a history of how the term and its cognates have been used and noted the confusion surrounding the terms. He returns frequently to a complaint voiced in a World Council of Churches (hereinafter WCC) 1954 publication, *Evangelism: The Mission of the Church to Those Outside Her Life*. It referred to a 1949 WCC study that had not accomplished much and said: "The slow progress seems to be due mainly to an almost chaotic confusion as to the meaning and scope of evangelism. Evangelism has indeed become the ecumenical theme par excellence, but we have hardly begun to make it a concern of serious ecumenical study."[2]

Barrett's study indicates that, despite a plethora of publications that include dozens of proposed definitions, serious terminological confusion remains. He suggests that many of the problems revolve around the question of whether evangelism means proclamation or whether it also includes the attainment of positive results.[3]

Most theologians in the twentieth century have not treated evangelism as a serious topic. Walter Klaiber says, "When one turns from the works of missiologists and specialists in evangelism to the textbooks for dogmatics, one encounters a curious hesitancy, if not a meaningful silence."[4] He briefly discusses publications by Karl Barth and Paul Tillich and then concludes, "Except for these two works no other common textbook in dogmatics or comparable work, as far as I can see, speaks of evangelism. Even the missionary task of the church as such is often only treated very briefly."[5]

In this study I present a theology of evangelism. I will give an account of Christian discipleship as a response to the reign of God. I then suggest that a more adequate definition of evangelism will focus on initiation into Christian discipleship. The relevance of this definition for questions of enculturation and its approach to persons of other religions will be examined. In the appendix I present a systemic approach to implementing these ideas in the ministry of a congregation.

To evangelize is one way of bearing witness to what God has done in Christ and is doing through the Holy Spirit today to convey the good news. One shares the message in both word and deed. Three of the Gospels and Acts record Jesus commanding a mission for his disciples. Matthew 28:19-20 says, "Go therefore and make disciples of all nations, baptizing them in the name of the Father and of the Son and of the Holy Spirit, and teaching them to obey everything that I have commanded you." Mark 16:15 says, "Go into all the world and proclaim the good news to the whole creation." In Luke 24:46-48 Jesus tells them, "Thus it is written, that the Messiah is to suffer and to rise from the dead on the third day, and that repentance and forgiveness of sins is to be proclaimed in his name to all nations, beginning from Jerusalem. You are witnesses of these things," which is followed by Acts 1:8 "But you will receive power when the Holy Spirit has come upon you; and you will be my witnesses in Jerusalem, in all Judea and Samaria, and to the ends of the earth." Without ignoring the important differences in the terminology of the three writers, one can say that these are different ways of describing the same task. To be a witness is to be a bearer of the gospel, the good news of the reign of God.

Yet the commands to "make disciples," "proclaim the good news," and "be [Christ's] witnesses," however important they may be for shaping the church's missionary activity, must be subordinate to the two commandments Christ called "the greatest." In the Judaism of his day, there was great confusion about how to prioritize the many commandments found in Scripture. When asked for his opinion, Jesus taught that Deuteronomy 6:5 and Leviticus 19:18 were the two texts on which the rest of Scripture (as recognized in his day) hung: "He said to them, 'You shall love the Lord your God with all your heart, and with all your soul, and with all your mind.' This is the greatest and first commandment. And a second is like it: 'You shall love your neighbor as yourself'" (Matt. 22:37-39). Central to the argument of this book is that the ministry of evangelism must always be grounded in the love of God and neighbor. For reasons that will be made clear in the argument of the whole book, grounding evangelism in the Great Commandments not only clarifies our understanding of this ministry but also shapes the criteria by which its adequacy is evaluated. If the whole of Christian life is to be understood as loving God and neighbor, then part of that love is the ministry of evangelism. And while one is evangelizing, one must always be motivated and guided by love.

Throughout Christian history serious problems have arisen when Christians have failed to hold together many different aspects of the Christian life. "Holistic" thus becomes a way of describing the approach to Christianity that includes many activities that sometimes appear contradictory. This book will seek to articulate a holistic understanding of evangelism that holds in tension at least six problem areas where the solution is a variation of "both . . . and" rather than "either . . . or." Evangelism must be seen as both a divine activity and a human activity. It must involve both invitation and the expectation of results, commonly referred to as proclamation and church growth. It must be aimed at a personal decision, but involve whole communities of persons. It must have its own integrity as a distinct ministry, yet be related to the other aspects of Christian discipleship, including education and spiritual formation. It must be discussed in the abstract and yet continually examined in particular contexts. And evangelism must never be understood in a way that is opposed to ministries of social justice.

One way of balancing all of these polarities is to understand evangelism as a ministry of Christian congregations. In the life of a congregation, all of these various aspects interact and overlap. A holistic understanding of evangelism is best understood as an interrelated set of practices in a congregational context. Hence, this book will focus on how congregations engage in evangelism since, it will be argued, all authentic evangelism requires initiation into the body of Christ in a specific Christian community and engagement with its life of worship, formation, and mission. There are many other ways to examine specific programs of evangelism. One could study evangelistic ministries that focus on personal testimony, use of electronic media, revivals, crusades, street preaching, and other methods. In specific contexts, these approaches may have significant value. But their evangelistic effectiveness always depends on how well they do one of two things. They either provide assistance to Christian congregations so they can better perform their ministries of evangelism, or they do on behalf of those congregations specific tasks they are unable to do for themselves.

William Abraham's *Logic of Evangelism* is the best account of a theology of evangelism published to date. He says, "We can best improve our thinking on evangelism by conceiving it as that set of intentional activities governed by the goal of initiating persons into the kingdom of God for the first time."[6]

At this initial stage, four advantages of this definition can be briefly elucidated. First, by using the word "intentional" Abraham has included both the activity of evangelism and pointed toward its desired result without requiring that result to be included in the activity. Barrett talked about two main groups of definitions of evangelism: those that focus on proclamation and those that really mean conversion. Abraham's definition includes the primary concerns of both groups of definitions. Second, this definition acknowledges that a wide range of activities should be included within evangelism. Many authors note that it must always be more than verbal, and Abraham's definition gives a way of including a "set of activities." Third, Abraham's reference to the "kingdom of God" underscores the priority of God's gracious action in the process of salvation.

Fourth, the focus on initiation does two things. It restricts the word "evangelism" to the beginning phase of the Christian life.

Some of the confusion surrounding this term and its cognates arises because the words are used to describe the whole process of helping individuals and cultures conform more fully to the will of God. The problem with such a broad usage is that it fails to offer a term for the particular ministry of helping persons enter into Christian discipleship. It helps our clarity of thought if we carefully distinguish a ministry of evangelism for that beginning stage, and then talk about Christian discipleship as the continuing growth toward Christian maturity that ought to follow the beginning steps.

This study seeks to refine Abraham's definition, and in chapter 4 we will return to it and revise it in light of the analysis offered in the first three chapters. Through this analysis I will be working out a rationale for the following definition: evangelism is that set of loving, intentional activities governed by the goal of initiating persons into Christian discipleship in response to the reign of God.

I have chosen to translate the New Testament phrase *basileia tou theou* as "reign of God." Many others, including Arias and Abraham, have used the traditional phrase "kingdom of God." Three reasons suggest that "reign of God" is preferable. First, "kingdom" has geographical implications that are too often associated with Christendom and the idea of Christian nations. Second, association with "king" reinforces stereotypes of God as male. Third, "Reign of God" carries connotations of God's active participation in the world. For these reasons I will use "reign" rather than "kingdom" except when quoting the work of others.

PART I

What Is Evangelism?

CHAPTER ONE

God's Evangelistic Love

To evangelize non-Christian persons without loving them fully is not to evangelize them well. To love non-Christian persons without evangelizing them is not to love them well. Loving God well means loving one's non-Christian neighbor evangelistically and evangelizing one's non-Christian neighbor lovingly.

The essential connections between loving God, loving one's neighbor, and doing evangelism are the fundamental insights that inform this book. Many Christians, especially those in the United States and Europe, are confused about evangelism. Some believe that loving their neighbors entails never inviting them to change their religion, whatever it is or is not. Some rightly point to the unloving ways in which so-called evangelism has been practiced, suggesting that such practices have no place in Christian ministry. They fail to see that not evangelizing such persons at all is also unloving.

Other Christians believe that gaining a non-Christian person's profession of faith, however obtained and with whatever follow-up, is the most important part of Christian ministry. They believe that eternal considerations are at stake, and that a person's entering into a saving relationship with Christ is the overriding issue.

They rightly point to the ways in which mission has sometimes become synonymous with social work, and interreligious dialogue has sometimes become religious syncretism, and they suggest that these practices so water down the gospel that it is hardly recognizable as the good news of God's reign preached by Jesus.

Hence, when some persons are invited to engage in the ministry of evangelism, they often enter into it with serious misunderstandings of what they should do and how they should do it. Others, influenced by stereotypes of practices in which they do not wish to engage, refrain from participating in anything that comes under the heading of evangelism. Many congregations emphasize that each Christian is called to be an evangelist. When such a claim is made, many members of those churches respond negatively. In some cases they do not believe it could possibly be true. Other members simply become very uncomfortable. Consequently, the question "What is evangelism?" takes on great significance. By clarifying the definition of the term, we can examine many aspects of the church's mission that we seek to identify under the label of evangelism.

The question received significant attention in the twentieth century. In his *Evangelize! A Historical Survey of the Concept*, David Barrett includes many other definitions offered over the years, and then concludes:

> This proliferation of definitions has in turn been denounced by major Christian organizations and gatherings as a situation of "bewildering variety," "almost chaotic confusion," and "a source of disturbing confusion among Christians." On closer inspection, however, almost all serious definitions that have been put down in black and white are found to be each reporting on only one or several of the multifold aspects of "evangelize," to be not incompatible but mutually compatible, and so collectively to form a vast body of cohesive interpretation on the concept of evangelization.
>
> To "evangelize" is in fact an immensely complex process made up of a large variety of elements. It is multifaceted, pluriform, inclusive, and comprehensive. The term "evangelize" and its cognates are therefore words of tremendous complexity, like all other words that are rich in meaning.[1]

Barrett is correct that many of the definitions overlap and are mutually compatible. When analyzed carefully, it becomes evident that many of them represent different ways of saying the same thing. At the same time, there are substantial differences that are worth thinking critically about. Barrett's discussion helps us realize that the words "evangelism" and "evangelization" have been used in a variety of ways. [2] He draws some distinctions about the cluster of meanings associated with each term, but his historical survey undercuts his conclusions. In my view, the terms are best understood to be interchangeable. Regardless of who uses the words, they are trying to describe the same activity of the church of Jesus Christ, and their different definitions and connotations are best taken as substantive disagreements about how the church engages in its ministry.

Greek Roots of "Evangelism"

Inquiring about evangelism is fundamentally related to inquiring about the gospel of Jesus Christ. The Greek word *euangelos* from which "evangelism" stems is normally translated as "gospel" in English Bibles. The prefix *eu* means good and *angelos* means news, so the gospel is the good news of Jesus Christ. The New Revised Standard Version, the New International Version, the King James Version, and the Revised Standard Version all use "Gospel" as the title of the first four books in the New Testament. The Greek for this is *euangelion*. This word is used more than sixty times in the Pauline and deutero-Pauline books of the New Testament. It frequently is used to describe the whole Christian message. For example, in Romans 1:1-3 Paul says, "Paul, a servant of Jesus Christ, called to be an apostle, set apart for the gospel of God, which he promised beforehand through his prophets in the holy scriptures, the gospel concerning his Son, who was descended from David according to the flesh." The same usage occurs in Romans 1:16-17 and 1 Corinthians 15:1-8. In each of these texts, *euangelion* is translated as "gospel" or "good news" in the NRSV.

The verbal form of this word, *euangelizesthai*, is used by Jesus many times. In Luke 4:43 he says, "I must proclaim the good news of the kingdom of God to the other cities also." In Matthew 11:5, Jesus says that one of the marks of his ministry is that "the poor have good news brought to them." In both cases the activity of communicating the good news is at the heart of this verb's meaning. In other places the NRSV uses the words "proclaim the gospel" (e.g., 1 Cor. 1:17). Gerhard Friedrich notes that in many cases εὐαγγελίζεσθαι is equivalent to κηρύσσειν, which means to preach.[3] However, there is a deeper connection between this activity of communicating the good news and everything else that the Christian community does. He says:

> εὐαγγελίζεσθαι is not just speaking and preaching; it is proclamation with full authority and power. Signs and wonders accompany the evangelical message. They belong together, for the Word is powerful and effective. The proclamation of the age of grace, of the rule of God, creates a healthy state in every respect. Bodily disorders are healed and man's relation to God is set right (Mt 4:23; 9:35; 11:5; Lk. 9:6; Ac. 8:4-8; 10:36 ff.; 14:8-18; 16:17 ff.; R. 15:16-20; 2 C. 12:12; Gl. 3:5). Joy reigns where this Word is proclaimed (Ac 8:8). It brings σωτηρία (1 C. 15:1 f.). It is the ὁδὸς σωτηρίας (Acts 16:17). It effects regeneration (1 Pt 1:23-25). It is not a word of man, but the living, eternal Word of God. The Holy Spirit, who was sought for the day of salvation, attests Himself now in the time of fulfillment when the glad tidings are proclaimed (1 Pt 1:12). Hence εὐαγγελίζεσθαι is to offer salvation. It is the powerful proclamation of the good news, the impartation of σωτηρία. This would be missed if εὐαγγελίζεσθαι were to take place in human fashion ἐν σοφίᾳ λόγου (1 C. 1:17).[4]

This brief word study from the New Testament helps explain two crucial characteristics of the discussion about evangelism in the twenty-first century. First, evangelism concerns matters that lie at the heart of Christianity. When evangelism is being discussed, the most central concerns of the faith are at stake. Clearly, questions about God and humanity are central in Christianity, and the question about the good news is Christianity's answer to how theology and anthropology intersect. Hence, any theology of evangelism should be deeply related to the doctrines of God, Christ, sin, justification, sanctification, ecclesiology, and all of the other loci of Christian theology.

Second, this look at the Greek roots explains the wide range of opinions regarding the nature and practice of evangelism. There are many widely varying versions of Christianity in the world—

many different churches, many different theological perspectives, and many different ways of being Christian. Each of these, either explicitly or implicitly, has an approach to evangelism embedded in its theology or its practices. Similarly, any theology of evangelism has theological commitments either stated or implied in the position. At the same time, the unity of Christ's church described in Ephesians 4:4-6—"one body . . . one Spirit . . . one hope . . . one Lord, one faith, one baptism, one God and Father of all"—drives us to engage each other in conversation about how best to understand and practice this dimension of the church's missionary activity.

Finding the Starting Point

How do we find the right beginning point for a theology of evangelism? A survey of recent literature reveals increasing clarity while offering a number of distinct alternatives.

Richard Stoll Armstrong's *Service Evangelism* begins with a theological analysis of faith. He argues that the evangelist's task is not to prove that Jesus Christ is the Son of God. He writes, "Our task is to show by the way we speak and act that we believe he is."[5] Armstrong then argues that the church should act as a servant of others. He goes on to define evangelism as

> reaching out to others in Christian love, identifying with them, caring for them, listening to them, and sharing one's faith with them in such a way that they will freely respond and want to commit themselves to trust, love and obey God as a disciple of Jesus Christ and a member of his servant community, the church. That, I realize, is a statement of method as well as my definition of evangelism. The word "service" is intended to imply a style of evangelism that is caring, supportive, unselfish, sensitive, and responsive to human need. It is evangelism done by a servant church, whose people are there not to be served but to serve.[6]

In this definition, evangelism focuses on meeting all of a person's needs, including spiritual needs.[7]

Malan Nel, in his article "Service and Evangelism: The Theology and Methodology of a Lifestyle," argues that Armstrong never intended service evangelism to be a method of accomplishing the task. Rather, it is a style "that has to do with the personality, character, commitment, and attitude of the evangelist."[8] Nel argues that Armstrong's approach to evangelism is built on an ecclesiology that sees the church as the servant of God.[9] Although the article talks more about style than theology, Nel clearly implies the centrality of a service ecclesiology for the practice of evangelism.

Ben Campbell Johnson's starting point in *Rethinking Evangelism: A Theological Approach* is self-consciously different. He discusses the "ghosts of eighteenth- and nineteenth-century evangelicalism" that still haunt the church. Partly to remedy this problem, he proposes a different starting point, saying:

> Without denying the intention of those who have begun their systematic quest with the doctrine of God, I believe a different starting point will yield a renewed perspective for evangelism and inspire methods appropriate for the task. I propose to begin a theology of evangelism with the Christian understanding of human beings. This approach may provide a needed corrective to the imperialistic style of evangelism we have deplored. We have already defined evangelism as an intentional outreach to persons, and so it would seem logical to begin our inquiry with the nature of persons—their needs, questions and desires. Evangelism must never end with only an exploration of human needs and questions, but perhaps this provides the best starting point.[10]

In other places, Johnson differentiates this approach from "a traditional approach from above," but then seeks to fuse the two together.[11] Despite what he says, it is not clear whether Johnson means to work from purely secular anthropologies or whether he seeks to begin with a Christian anthropology that originates from Scripture. He does both in chapter 2. Part of his analysis relies on the work of Jung, Maslow, and Berger and Luckmann. Another section relies on a traditional exegetical approach to anthropology, but there is little connection between the two analyses. However, the question that Johnson is addressing remains extremely important. It is clear that our theology of evangelism must take the human subject with utmost seriousness and make sure that our answers are correlated with humanity's questions.

In many respects, a variety of different theologies of evangelism is beneficial for precisely the reason articulated by Johnson. A variety of perspectives gives the best opportunity for seeing the many different sides and facets of the gospel and its communication to the world. Harry Poe's survey of the different ways the gospel has been construed demonstrates the importance of these central ideas in the thinking of many theologians throughout Christian history. Poe sees a virtue in this diversity, arguing "the different elements of the gospel speak to different levels of spiritual concern in different cultures at different times."[12]

Two of the best theological books about evangelism begin with its relationship to the reign of God. Mortimer Arias, William Abraham, and others give us an essential insight when they make the reign of God a central theme in understanding the gospel. In part the centrality of this theme is made clear by the etymology of the word itself. For Christians, the Bible should be the primary locus for discerning how the gospel is best understood. Arias and Abraham follow many New Testament scholars who argue that the proclamation of the kingdom of God is central to Jesus' whole ministry. Further, many argue that the preaching and teaching of the apostles centered on the reign of God and that our witness today should still focus on how it is "at hand" in the world and how it is to be anticipated as coming fully in the future.

Arias uses the kingdom of God as a way of bringing the insights of liberation theology and other movements for social justice into the center of the church's evangelistic ministry. He argues "Jesus' evangelization, then, was *kingdom evangelization*."[13] Arias goes on to argue that the message of the kingdom has continued to be present in the church, but it has been eclipsed. It has remained as a "subversive memory."[14] In recovering this subversive memory, the church will resolve its current crisis with regard to evangelization. He perceives a crisis in the credibility, motivation, definition, and methods of evangelization. In response to this crisis he puts forth an understanding of evangelization that he describes as "biblical, evangelical, holistic, humanizing, conscientizing, liberating, contextual, engaged, incarnational and conflictive."[15] For him, each of these is "a natural component of evangelization in the perspective of the kingdom."[16]

Arias adopts an understanding of the kingdom that had become standard in much of modern New Testament interpretation and theology. Jesus clearly proclaimed that the reign of God is at hand, and yet he also spoke of its coming with power in the future. Arias says, "There is an unbearable tension in Jesus' proclamation of the kingdom. The kingdom has come—and will come. The time is fulfilled—but we await the consummation. The kingdom is experience—but it is also hope. It is present and imminent. It is 'already' and 'not yet.'"[17]

Arias then makes reference to Oscar Cullmann's analogy of the difference between World War II's D day when the defeat of German forces was assured and VE day when the Nazis finally surrendered.[18]

The perspective of the kingdom of God shapes Arias's discussion of evangelization in several ways. From one point of view, the kingdom is seen as a gift, imparting forgiveness and reconciliation. At the same time the kingdom is hope. "To evangelize is to announce the coming kingdom, the kingdom of peace and justice, of love and life, the consummation of God's purpose of love with humanity and his universe—to announce the undefeatable fulfillment of creation."[19] Announcing the kingdom as hope also includes the ministry of denunciation. Evangelization must "denounce anything, any power, any program, any trend which opposes God's purpose for humanity."[20] Evangelization must side with the poor, the marginalized, and the powerless in their struggle for liberation from the demonic powers of this world. This kind of evangelization invites persons to respond with a costly discipleship. Arias says:

> Discipleship evangelization, then, means recruitment—an invitation to participate in the blessings of the kingdom, to celebrate the hopes of the kingdom, and to engage in the tasks of the kingdom. It means recruitment to discipleship *in* the kingdom and *for* the kingdom.
>
> We need to correct the almost-invincible tendency of our evangelization to present the gospel in terms of "blessings"—benefits to be received, answers to all our questions, remedy to all our evils, new life to be enjoyed, a future state to be secured—without at the same time presenting the challenges, demands, and tasks of the kingdom. We need to remember Bonhoeffer's warning about reducing "costly discipleship" to "cheap grace."[21]

From this perspective, then, conversion means giving one's allegiance to the kingdom.[22] Arias critiques the view that conversion is a personalized, privatized transaction between God and the soul. He says it is only by refocusing our thinking on Jesus' proclamation of the in-breaking and radically transforming reign of God that we can fully regain a biblical and holistic understanding of evangelism.

In a similar way William Abraham effectively uses the present-but-still-coming reign of God as the focal point for evangelism, and he argues for a new Christian catechesis focusing on six aspects of life under God's reign. He argues that if the ministry of Jesus and the apostles was focused on the kingdom, then our ministry today should likewise be focused in the same way. He makes a sweeping claim:

> Any considered attempt to develop a coherent concept of evangelism that will be serviceable in the present must begin with eschatology. Whatever evangelism may be, it is at least intimately related to the gospel of the reign of God that was inaugurated in the life, death, and resurrection of Jesus of Nazareth. Any vision of evangelism that ignores the kingdom of God, or relegates it to a position of secondary importance, or fails to wrestle thoroughly with its content is destined at the outset to fail. This is so because the kingdom of God is absolutely central to the ministry of Jesus and to the mission of the disciples that launched the Christian movement into history. What is not at stake here is the prevalence of the idea of the kingdom of God in the biblical writings, although that could be argued persuasively. What is at stake is the fundamental theological horizon within which both Jesus and his followers conceive and carry out the first, and paradigmatic, evangelistic action of the church. This cannot be the last word but rather must be the first word on evangelism.[23]

These words in Abraham's *Logic of Evangelism* open the chapter entitled "The Gospel." It is clear that for Abraham, the reign of God is precisely the heart of the gospel and that is why it constitutes the "fundamental theological horizon" shaping evangelistic practice.

Abraham gives an account of the kingdom as already here and yet to come. He argues that the early Christian community experienced the sovereign hand of God in their midst, and that this provided their primary motivation for evangelism.[24] He says, "In other words, evangelism was rooted in a corporate experience of the rule of God that provided not only the psychological strength and support that was clearly needed in a hostile environment but that also signified the active presence of God in their midst."[25]

Arias and Abraham have made a very significant and important point about the significance of the reign of God for a holistic understanding of the gospel, and thus of evangelism. Christian discipleship is a faithful response to the reign of God. Christian discipleship includes believing the gospel, faithfully accepting the relationship God offers, and obediently following God's will in all matters great and small. Arias is right that a re-emphasis on the reign of God will counteract some of the distortions brought to contemporary Christianity by an individualistic form of Protestantism. Christians must remember that God's will embraces all of creation and that the reign of God includes justice in political, economic, and cultural spheres as well as in the eternal life of individuals.

Both Abraham and Arias are right that basing evangelism on the reign of God will provide a more holistic approach that will heal many of the problems evangelism has faced in the last two centuries. Abraham's arguments for the role of divine action in eschatology and the role of the Holy Spirit in bringing about the reign of God are especially important.

On what basis should one select a starting point for a theology of evangelism? I believe that two considerations should govern this choice. Because evangelism is so strongly connected to the gospel, both etymologically and substantively, a theology of evangelism should begin with that which is most fundamental to the gospel. It should be so fundamental that it is arguably the aspect of the gospel on which all else depends. It should be so central that no single aspect of the gospel could be fully understood without reference to it. Second, it should reciprocally allow for all the other parts of the message to take their proper places in the theological structure. The beginning point in one's theological construal of evangelism should thus help shape all that follows.

For these reasons one's theology of evangelism ought to hinge on how one construes the message of the Bible. David Kelsey in his *Uses of Scripture in Recent Theology* makes the case that it is analytically true that any text called "scripture" is understood to be whole.[26] Wholeness is the pattern that the reader, whether it is a theologian or a church in its doctrine, discerns in the text. When the text is read in the light of that pattern, its various parts are all seen to be functioning toward a certain end. Either implicitly or explicitly, Christians read the Bible as having a general tenor or theme that holds all of it together. Since the gospel is an important part of the New Testament's message, if not the constitutive center of that message, then how that gospel is understood and communicated to non-Christians is integrally related to one's understanding of the wholeness of Scripture.[27] It is highly unlikely that all Christians will agree on one understanding of this general tenor of Scripture. Indeed, Poe may be right in valuing a plurality of readings. It is true that many readings of Scripture are possible. Indeed, the wide variety of perspectives, literary styles, and theologies in the sixty-six books of the Bible make such a plurality of interpretations inevitable. The diversity of such readings is also positive and helpful for methodology because it reminds us that God is far beyond our understanding. Seeing God and seeing God's mission is best done by offering a variety of readings of the text.

God's Love as the Central Theme of Scripture

Walter Klaiber has offered an interpretation of the gospel in the New Testament. In *Call and Response: Biblical Foundations of a Theology of Evangelism* he contends that there are three basic forms of the New Testament message: "the 'gospel of the kingdom' of the Jesus tradition as the Synoptic Gospels hand it down; the 'word of the cross' of the Pauline gospel; and the witness of the 'incarnation of the Word of God' which determines the message of the Gospel of John and other early Christian traditions."[28] Klaiber notes the diversity of these three versions and suggests that it is not surprising, given the nature of the texts. He says:

> The New Testament is not a missionary writing in which the fundamental gospel is presented with a consistent orientation towards a certain circle of listeners or in the most generalized form possible. It is a collection of writings for certain churches which cite this basic missional gospel in very different situations and utilize it for theological or teaching purposes; thereby, they obviously also reach back to fundamental forms of this gospel

which were different from the very beginning. Nonetheless a unity is recognizable.[29]

Klaiber understands that the task of evangelism is to bring this recognizable center into contact with real human beings who live in different contexts than those that were addressed by the New Testament's authors. In trying to describe this center he says,

> The basis and power of this message lies in the certainty that "God is for us," which is guaranteed by Jesus' message and his offering of his life for us. The reality of God's proexistence reaches human need in its entire complexity and breaks through the power of sin which draws its power from the isolation and egocentricity of humankind.
>
> The mission of the church of Jesus Christ, whose witness, communion, and ministry is filled and formed by God's existence *for us*, is grounded in this. The message is, however, also above all the basis and content of the evangelism in which the church inwardly and outwardly names and bears witness to that from which it lives and which delivers human kind: God's merciful care in Jesus Christ.[30]

Klaiber here argues that the gospel is rooted in God's gracious, saving love for humankind. That love then interacts with human need in all of its complexity.

Klaiber's analysis of three different forms of the gospel is overly generalized. He does not give a sufficient account of how the reign of God is related to the word of the cross in the Pauline and deutero-Pauline literature. Yet it points us to another alternative. His conclusion points to a synthesis where the love of God is the fundamental category and the reign of God is the expression of that love.

Another reason the reign of God is not the beginning point for a theology of evangelism is that it is not the most fundamental theological category. The reign of God—expressed both in the Old Testament with its emphasis on God's election of Israel and the New Tesament's teaching of the coming of Christ—is best understood as an expression of God's love. We have argued in preceding chapters that God's most important attribute is love. It is God's nature to love, both in the intra-trinitarian life and in the Triune God's love for

God's creation. Why does God care enough to reign? Why does God announce the coming of that reign in the person of Jesus? Why does Christ die for the redemption of the world? Why does God guarantee the fulfillment of all these promises in a new heaven and new earth? The answer to all these and other fundamental questions lies in God's essence, which is love. God creates, redeems, and saves the world because God is love. God loves the world.

My argument construes God's evangelistic love of the world as the central message of Scripture. God creates the world out of love, God judges the world's sin out of love, and God is actively saving the world because of that same love. The good news is that, despite all appearances to the contrary, God's love has triumphed over all the powers of evil in the world. Human beings are invited to respond to that love by accepting God's offer of a relationship and all of the new possibilities that offer entails.

Central to any understanding of the Bible's teaching is a description of who God is. The Old and New Testaments contain many images of God and characterizations of what God is like. Theologians have often summarized these by discussing God's attributes. Often an account of the divine attributes includes the following: omnipresence, omniscience, sovereignty, justice, mercy, and love.

God Is Love

The Wesleyan tradition emphasizes that love is God's most basic attribute. This is a theological conclusion arising out of and shaping the tradition's reading of Scripture. One of the most important biblical texts in this reading is 1 John 4:7-12. This is primarily an argument for Christians to love one another, but the warrant for the exhortation is that God is love.

> Beloved, let us love one another, because love is from God; everyone who loves is born of God and knows God. Whoever does not love does not know God, for God is love. God's love was revealed among us in this way: God sent his only Son into the world so that we might live through him. In this is love, not that we loved God but that he loved us and sent his Son to be the atoning sacrifice for our sins. Beloved, since God loved us so much, we also ought to love one another. No one has ever seen God; if we love one another, God lives in us, and his love is perfected in us.

God is love, and those who abide in love abide in God, and God abides in them. Love has been perfected among us in this: that we may have boldness on the day of judgment, because as he is, so are we in this world. There is no fear in love, but perfect love casts out fear; for fear has to do with punishment, and whoever fears has not reached perfection in love. We love because he first loved us. (1 John 4:7-12, 16b-19)

Regarding verse 8, "God is love," John Wesley said, "This little sentence brought St. John more sweetness, even in the time he was writing it, than the whole world can bring. God is often styled holy, righteous, wise; but not holiness, righteousness, or wisdom in the abstract, as he is said to be love; intimating that this is his darling, his reigning attribute, the attribute that sheds an amiable glory on all his other perfections."[31] This text offers us an organizing theme for the whole of Scripture. It makes explicit reference to the incarnation of Christ as an action of God's love. It then suggests that Christians ought to live their lives in response to this love.

There are at least two ways in which a focus on the love of God presents a coherent account of the wholeness of Scripture. First, it offers clear ties to many other places in the Bible where the love of God is mentioned. The Old Testament frequently describes God as the one who steadfastly loves humanity. The term "steadfast love," usually translating the Hebrew word *hesed*, shows up more than 170 times in the NRSV of the Old Testament. It appears in nineteen of the thirty-nine books. In Genesis 24:12 Abraham's servant prays that God would show Abraham steadfast love. Exodus records that God told Moses on Mount Sinai:

> The Lord passed before him, and proclaimed,
>   "The LORD, the LORD,
>   a God merciful and gracious,
>   slow to anger,
>   and abounding in steadfast love and faithfulness,
>   keeping steadfast love for the thousandth generation,
>   forgiving iniquity and transgression and sin,
>   yet by no means clearing the guilty,
>   but visiting the iniquity of the parents
>   upon the children
>   and the children's children,
>   to the third and the fourth generation." (Exod. 34:6-7)

Psalm 136 uses "for his steadfast love endures forever" as the last line in each of the twenty-six verses. God's steadfast love is perhaps the dominant theme of the book of Hosea. The Gospel of John says, "For God so loved the world that he gave his only Son, so that everyone who believes in him may not perish but may have eternal life" (3:16).

The focus on the love of God as the central theme of Scripture has a second and perhaps more profound advantage. It serves well as the most basic way of understanding who God is and all of the ways God is described in the Bible. It makes sense of God's essence and of God's activities as creator, judge, and savior.

Christian doctrine teaches that the only way to make sense of the various accounts of God's essence in Scripture is to speak of one God in three persons, that is, the Trinity. Deuteronomy 6:4 says that God is one. In addition, God is one with Christ, and the Holy Spirit is God as well. The doctrine of the Trinity says that God is, in God's essence, a community of persons loving Godself.[32]

The Bible characteristically shows little interest in a philosophical account of God's essence. Typically, God is described by God's actions. Nevertheless, at two key points, God's essence is described more abstractly and absolutely. The first comes in Exodus 3 where Moses confronts God in the burning bush on the holy mountain and asks for God's name. At that point, "God said to Moses, 'I AM WHO I AM.' He said further, 'Thus you shall say to the Israelites, "I AM has sent me to you"'" (3:14). This text provides an etymology for the divine name YHWH by linking it to the Hebrew word *hayah*, which means "to be." Christian theologians and philosophers for centuries have taken this as a text that suggests God is the one who is self-existent. When Scripture opens, there is no account of how God came to be. God is. God is the "I AM." In the words of Revelation 22:13, "I am the Alpha and the Omega, the first and the last, the beginning and the end."

Yet, God's existence is always characterized by God's love. The second crucial text describing God's essence is the passage noted above in 1 John that says "God is love." The love that is at the heart of God's essence is expressed in this Exodus 3 passage as well. God is the "I AM," who is then immediately identified as the one who has been in relationship with Moses' people. God says, "Thus you shall say to the Israelites, 'The LORD, the God of your ancestors, the God of Abraham, the God of Isaac, and the God of Jacob, has sent me to you': / This is my name forever, / and this my title for all generations" (3:15). God's essence is to be in relationship.

God's love is also fundamental to understanding God's creative activity. The opening verses of the Bible describe God creating a world and calling it good. In contrast with the other creation myths current in the ancient Near East, God's creative activity is not the result of a cosmic conflict between good and evil or between any other opposing forces. The one God chooses to make a world and calls it good. God's creative power is attested in the Psalms and in the Wisdom literature. God's concern for God's creation underlies much of the theology of the New Testament. Paul knows that the creation is beloved by God and that the redemption that is in Christ will benefit the whole world. He says, "For the creation waits with eager longing for the revealing of the children of God; for the creation was subjected to futility, not of its own will but by the will of the one who subjected it, in hope that the creation itself will be set free from its bondage to decay and will obtain the freedom of the glory of the children of God" (Rom. 8:19-21).

God's work is described in the New Testament as a type of re-creation. Ephesians says, "With all wisdom and insight he has made known to us the mystery of his will, according to his good pleasure that he set forth in Christ, as a plan for the fullness of time, to gather up all things in him, things in heaven and things on earth" (Eph. 1:8*b*-10). Colossians sees Christ as "the firstborn of all creation" in whom "all things hold together." It continues, "For in him all the fullness of God was pleased to dwell, and through him God was pleased to reconcile to himself all things, whether on earth or in heaven, by making peace through the blood of his cross" (Col. 1:15, 17, 19-20). Revelation describes "a new heaven and a new earth; for the first heaven and the first earth had passed away" (Rev. 21:1).

God's activities as judge are also best understood in the context of the covenantal relationship that God has with humanity in general and with Israel in particular. When human beings violate those basic relational expectations, God judges what has gone wrong and condemns the people for their sins. This is best understood as an expression of God's love. Whether it is worshiping other gods,[33] mistreating aliens in their midst,[34] or failing to care for widows,[35] human sins are contrary to human well-being, and God tells the people that they need to change. Isaiah's judgment in chapter 1 makes God's case that Israel's sins constitute a broken relationship.

> The ox knows its owner,
> and the donkey its master's crib;
> but Israel does not know,
> my people do not understand.
> Ah, sinful nation,
> people laden with iniquity,
> offspring who do evil,
> children who deal corruptly,
> who have forsaken the LORD,
> who have despised the Holy One of Israel,
> who are utterly estranged! (Isa. 1:3-4)

Then, in Romans, Paul ascribes sin to all of humanity. Each person is guilty.[36]

Yet, God's judgment aims at restoring humanity's relationship with God and concomitantly at restoring human flourishing. One way to understand the Ten Commandments is to see some of them as the keys to how human community can be sustained.[37] The prophets condemned economic oppression of the poor, saying, "[Joining] house to house" and adding "field to field, until there is room for no one" else is wrong (Isa. 5:8).[38] The laws in the Torah explicitly protect aliens, widows, and orphans (Exod. 22:21-24). God's judgment is aimed at human well-being and it includes all persons. Given the tendencies of human sin, it specifically focuses on those who are marginalized in various ways.

The intended outcome of judgment is a restored relationship to God and to other human beings. Joel makes the offer of salvation clear, repeating a phrase found in Psalms and other texts:

> Yet even now, says the LORD,
> return to me with all your heart,
> with fasting, with weeping, and with mourning;
> rend your hearts and not your clothing.
> Return to the LORD, your God,

> for he is gracious and merciful,
>> slow to anger, and abounding in steadfast love,
>>> and relents from punishing. (Joel 2:12-13)[39]

God's concern for justice and vindication is a frequent theme in Scripture (e.g., Ps. 103:6). Micah 3 focuses on it. The *Magnificat* in Luke celebrates God's acts of lifting up the lowly, bringing down the powerful, and filling the hungry with good things (Luke 1:52-53). God's vision is of a world where everyone is in a right relationship with God. God's actions are intended to bless all the peoples of the earth, and all are to worship on Mount Zion. The violence and sin that have destroyed human well-being shall end. Indeed, God's peace will recreate the kind of world God intended in the first place. Isaiah looks for the time when "they will not hurt or destroy on all my holy mountain; / for the earth will be full of the knowledge of the LORD / as the waters cover the sea" (Isa. 11:9). The prophet Micah articulates this universal vision clearly. He sees that the temple in Jerusalem shall be lifted up and many nations will come there to learn and worship.

> For out of Zion shall go forth instruction,
>> and the word of the LORD from Jerusalem.
> He shall judge between many peoples,
>> and shall arbitrate between strong nations far away;
> they shall beat their swords into plowshares,
>> and their spears into pruning hooks;
> nation shall not lift up sword against nation,
>> neither shall they learn war any more;
> but they shall all sit under their own vines and under their own
>> fig trees,
>> and no one shall make them afraid;
>> for the mouth of the LORD of hosts has spoken.
>>> (Micah 4:2c-4)

The prophetic vision of God's desire for Israel and all the peoples of the earth is stated in many different ways in the Old Testament, but the general direction is always the same. God intends to restore all of humanity to a right relationship with God, and, so restored, they should worship God and live in right relationships with each other.

Incarnation—the Sending of the Son

From the perspective of the Christian Scripture, the key turning point in God's mission was the sending of the Son into the world. John's Prologue describes the Word of God as "the true light, which enlightens everyone," and in Christ it came into the world. The purpose of this coming was that to those "who believed in his name, he gave power to become children of God" (John 1:12). The sending of the Son was for the purpose of saving the world (John 3:17). Philippians 2:5-11 portrays Christ entering into the world and being obedient to the point of death on a cross. God then exalted him with the purpose that everyone should acknowledge him as Lord to the glory of God the Father. Then the author of Colossians says, "For in him all the fullness of God was pleased to dwell, and through him God was pleased to reconcile to himself all things, whether on earth or in heaven, by making peace through the blood of his cross" (Col. 1:19-20).

In his ministry on earth Christ proclaimed the coming of God's reign. He broke the boundaries that typically separated persons by gender, nationality, social class, or the appearance of righteousness. He showed the righteousness of God and declared that faith would lead to salvation. He gathered a new community and gave them new ceremonies to remember his ministry. He reinterpreted the law in order to maintain its spiritual purpose rather than a bare following of its letter. At the end of his ministry, he promised that God would send an advocate who would continue to guide the community. In Christ's sacrificial death on the cross Christians see the atonement for the sins of the world. In Christ's resurrection they see the firstfruits of a resurrection to all who believe in Christ.

The proclamation of the reign of God was the primary content of Jesus' message as conveyed in the Synoptic Gospels. Matthew 4:17 and Mark 1:15 suggest that this was the message he preached at the start of his public ministry. The parables of the reign of God describe God's purposes. Similarly, the apocalyptic element of Paul's preaching was an important part of his proclamation of the gospel. Other New Testament writers have different understandings of the reign of God, but it is a significant aspect of the whole canon.

Klaiber summarizes Paul's missionary preaching as showing

> a double aspect of the gospel. Both characteristics, however, do
> not stand unrelated next to one another; rather they are closely
> connected with each other:
> (1) The gospel as the message of God's activity in Jesus Christ
> reports about God's reconciling work in Jesus' cross and
> resurrection.
> (2) The gospel as the inauguration of salvation makes faithfulness
> unto salvation present for everyone who hears and accepts the
> message.[40]

The reign of God as preached by Jesus is fulfilled by Christ's death
and resurrection. Paul's preaching of the "word of the cross" com-
plements the preaching of God's reign in the Gospels. Romans
1:16-17 leads to Romans 14:17, which then leads to Colossians
1:13.[41]

David Bosch's analysis of the apostolic paradigm of Christianity
argues that one of the crucial issues facing the first-century
Christian community was how to relate the Gentile mission with
the original mission to the Jewish people. While there are different
nuances in each of the subparadigms he analyzes, a decisive factor
is that Jesus himself was crossing boundaries in his ministry all the
time. Bosch says, "What is it that gave rise to the many sayings,
parables, and stories that seem at the very least, to nourish the idea
that, one day, God's covenant will reach far beyond the people of
Israel? In my view there can be no doubt: the primary inspiration
for all these stories could only have been the provocative, boundary-
breaking nature of Jesus' own ministry."[42]

The Sending of the Holy Spirit

David Bosch points out that until the sixteenth century, the word
"mission" was used exclusively "with reference to the doctrine of
the Trinity, that is, of the sending of the Son by the Father and of the
Holy Spirit by the Father and the Son."[43] During the first century,
an important way of seeing God as Triune was captured in the bap-
tismal formula in Matthew 28:20. In Acts 2, the Holy Spirit
descends with power and the miracles of Pentecost occur. From

that time on, the book of Acts records miracles, powerful preaching, and the spread of the gospel throughout the Roman Empire.

Bosch suggests that one of Luke's greatest contributions is the focus on the role of the Spirit in mission. In the Gospel the Spirit is promised. In volume two—the book of Acts—the Spirit comes with power. Pentecost, described in chapter 2, is the fulfillment of Jesus' promise that the disciples will be given power if they wait in Jerusalem. The promised power is first and foremost the power to become a new community—a community embracing the diversity of the Jewish diaspora. It was also a power that both permitted and required the spread of the gospel geographically and ethnically into the Gentile world. All of this is attributed to the working of the Holy Spirit. The gift of the Spirit to Gentiles authorizes their baptism and eventually supports the decision made at the Jerusalem Council in Acts 15. According to this account, the Holy Spirit led the leaders of the church in Jerusalem to welcome Gentile converts as brothers and sisters without imposing the burdens of circumcision and observing the dietary laws (Acts 15:23-29).

The work of the Holy Spirit is described somewhat differently in John's Gospel. There, Christ promises a *paraklātos*—often translated as "advocate," "counselor," or "comforter."[44] But one of the crucial clues to understanding what John means by this term is that it is another *paraklātos*—one who is like Jesus. The Spirit will remind the disciples of Jesus' teaching and lead them into all truth. In John 20:22 Jesus breathes on the disciples and says "receive the Holy Spirit."

God's Grace Is Offered to All

One of the crucial dimensions of this view of God's gracious activity is that it has been and is being offered to every human being. Describing Christ, John 1:9 says, "the true light, which enlightens everyone, was coming into the world." Numerous additional New Testament passages indicate that God is reaching out to persons who have not actually heard the gospel preached. According to Acts, Paul's sermon in Athens makes reference to the altar to an unknown God. Paul chose to make contact with the Athenians by starting with one of the religions already present in that culture. In this account he says, "What therefore you worship as unknown, this I proclaim to you. The God who made the world and everything in it, he who is Lord of heaven and earth, does not live in shrines made by human hands, nor is he served by human hands, as though he needed anything, since he himself gives to all mortals life and breath and all things" (Acts 17:23-25). Further, in Romans Paul argues that some sort of knowledge of God is available to all persons.

> For what can be known about God is plain to them, because God has shown it to them. Ever since the creation of the world his eternal power and divine nature, invisible though they are, have been understood and seen through the things he has made. So they are without excuse; for though they knew God, they did not honor him as God or give thanks to him, but they became futile in their thinking, and their senseless minds were darkened. (Rom. 1:19-21)

At the same time, Christ's statement in John 14:6 that "no one comes to the Father except through me" raises the issue of how persons who have not heard Christ preached can come to salvation. Paul also raises the question, saying, "But how are they to call on one in whom they have not believed? And how are they to believe in one of whom they have never heard? And how are they to hear without someone to proclaim him? And how are they to proclaim him unless they are sent? . . . So faith comes from what is heard, and what is heard comes through the word of Christ" (Rom. 10:14-17).

The question of whether there is any natural knowledge of God apart from revelation has a long and controverted history in Christian theology. The idea that any natural knowledge could also be saving knowledge has been widely rejected. Another alternative suggestion is that all persons have been given a supernatural knowledge of God through prevenient grace. This would include persons who have not heard the gospel preached. Many texts of Scripture lead us to believe that God wills all persons to be saved. On some readings, God's justice requires that everyone be given a chance for salvation. The question of their salvation then depends on whether human beings respond in faith to whatever contact with God's grace they have.

The Reign of God and Christian Discipleship

All of the above actions taken by God are expressions of God's love for humanity. They are evangelistic in two senses. First, God's actions are good news. Humanity's problems can be solved, and God is actively working to do that. Racism, sexism, hunger, war, sexual immorality, disease, and even the power of death are being overcome. God has won the decisive battle and eventually the war will be won as well.

Second, these actions are invitational, because God is continually working in the world to invite and encourage persons to participate in the reign of God. This is also true of social structures, where God seeks to end the larger, corporate patterns of human behavior that are destructive of life and human flourishing. In a sense, God is always inviting the world to embrace God's reign and return to the set of relationships God intends for it.

Finally, it should be noted that the reign of God is not coextensive with the church. God will save those whom God will save. God is seeking to recreate the world so that God's purposes are accomplished. Hence, God is active in places where there are no Christians. Further, there are Christians who are actually working against God's purposes. Thus, while the church is God's chief instrument, it is not God's only instrument.

CHAPTER TWO

Humanity's Evangelistic Love of God and Neighbor

J esus understood much of his ministry to be centered on announcing and proclaiming the "good news" of the reign of God. It is highly significant that, in Mark's Gospel, Jesus begins his ministry with this announcement right after his baptism (Mark 1:15). Matthew and Luke place the announcement early in Jesus' ministry as well (Matt. 4:17, Luke 4:43). The good news comes to persons as the manifestation of God's grace. Yet, as the New Testament describes the encounters of specific individuals with that grace, it is striking how many different ways it occurs.

Sometimes grace is costly, having the appearance of bad news. For the money changers in the temple, the announcement that they had profaned the Lord's house was presumably not very welcome news (Matt. 21:12-13, Mark 11:15-19, Luke 19:45-48, John 2:13-17). For Zacchaeus, the restoration of his relationship to God and to the people of Israel required great financial sacrifice. He promised to give half of his possessions to the poor and to restore fourfold whatever he had taken fraudulently from persons. Jesus' response was to proclaim that salvation had come to Zacchaeus's house that day (Luke 19:8-9). The rich young man's love of possessions prevented him from receiving the same grace (Matt. 19:16-30, Mark 10:17-31, Luke 18:18-30).

Other times grace comes to the person as meeting an obvious physical need. For those who were ill, it came as healing. The woman who had suffered from hemorrhages for twelve years with the resulting perception of ritual impurity was healed and told, "Take heart, daughter, your faith has made you well" (Matt. 9:22). To the blind beggar Jesus said, "Receive your sight; your faith has saved you" (Luke 18:43). In both of these instances, the Greek verb *sozo* is used. With the woman it is translated as "physical healing," and with the blind man there is a double meaning of both healing and freeing from sin. Jesus' response to the paralytic in Mark 2:1-12 is first to forgive his sins and then to enable him to walk.

Other times there is an immediate emotional crisis to which grace responds. The jailer in Philippi discovered that his prisoners had not escaped, and instead of committing suicide he discovered God's grace (Acts 16:25-34). While the textual evidence for John 7:53–8:11 is mixed, many scholars believe it is an authentic account of Jesus' ministry.[1] The woman caught in adultery is about to be stoned, but instead, she is rescued from capital punishment and receives forgiveness. Jesus tells her, "Go your way, and from now on do not sin again" (John 8:11). The Samaritan woman at the well responded to Jesus' willingness to reach out to her. He was not concerned about the reasons for her five husbands and present relationship. He did care enough to break the conventional boundaries and offer her living water. He engages her in conversation about key theological issues. She recognizes him as the Messiah and becomes the witness through whom the people in her village are brought to faith in Christ.[2]

In other cases, grace appears to answer the spiritual longings of the person involved. Nicodemus was told that he needed to be "born from above," or "born anew" (John 3:3).[3] We are not told how he responded, but he was later involved in the burial of Jesus (John 3:1-15, 19:39). The Ethiopian eunuch was seeking to understand the Scriptures, and under Philip's tutelage he saw that Jesus was the Christ (Acts 8:26-40). Second Timothy pictures Paul's younger colleague as someone who had been familiar with the "sacred writings" of Judaism from childhood and who now has the "sincere faith" that previously dwelt in his grandmother and mother. We are not given the details, but it is probable that Timothy was raised to be a Christian from childhood.

In each of these cases, God's grace came through words and deeds that met the person's deepest needs and offered that person salvation. Yet what is also significant is the diversity of ways in which God's grace was experienced. This points again to the fundamental reality of God's love. Love considers how to care for the beloved. The beloved's needs shape the concrete ways in which that love is offered. The reign of God is best understood as that state where all of God's creatures are fully loved. This leads to the diversity of ways in which the reign of God comes to individuals. For the sick it is healing. But their needs, in most cases, involve more than healing of the body, and the coming of the reign of God addresses spiritual needs as well. Thus, physical healing may include restoration to the community, forgiveness of sins, restoration of spiritual growth, or a call to new service.

Thus, whatever a person's primary need, the reign of God always involves God's effort to love the person, restoring the person to his or her full humanity. God desires that each person fulfill the potential which God intended in creation. The good news is that the bad news is temporary. The power of evil and the existence of sin and its terrible consequences are real. Yet, God has defeated them, and they are not the final answer. God reigns, and the fulfillment of God's reign is coming. Part of the ministry of evangelism is, in Mortimar Arias's phrase, "announcing the reign of God." It is reminding the world that all of the forces that destroy life are wrong, and in an ultimate sense, they have already lost. Walter Brueggemann insists that how we frame this announcement is important. He says that the announcement has many different formulations in Scripture. But, "the announcement in our context of faith and ministry must, in my judgment, be concrete, uncompromising and christological. Thus, the lean announcement is that in Jesus Christ, God has overcome the power, threat, and attraction of the power of death."[4]

47

Faith as a Response to Grace

The appropriate human response to God's grace is faith. One key New Testament text sums up this relationship. Ephesians 2:8-10 says, "For by grace you have been saved through faith, and this is not your own doing; it is the gift of God—not the result of works, so that no one may boast. For we are what he has made us, created in Christ Jesus for good works, which God prepared beforehand to be our way of life." This is not simply a Pauline gloss on Christianity that is out of step with the rest of Scripture. Rather, Paul is describing first the priority of God's grace, and then the human response of acceptance that is faith. This same pattern appears in Jesus' ministry when he heals those who respond in faith and does not perform miracles where he does not find faith. John 3:16 is another key text that talks about God's love for the world and the offer of salvation to all those who believe in Christ.

One of the problems faced by English-speaking readers of the New Testament is the language's separation of "to believe," "belief," and "faith" as if they were unrelated concepts. Too often "believe" is understood as something that has to do with emotions and commitment, that is, involving a degree of tenacity with which one gives assent. "Belief" is construed too frequently as an intellectual proposition separated from daily life. "Faith" then becomes a network of positions that one possesses.

Knowledge of the Greek words is helpful here. The words "faith," "belief," and "to believe" are the English words commonly used to translate the Greek *pistis*, and *pisteuō*. While both words have the same root, the noun has the typical *-is* ending and the verb the *euō* ending for the first-person singular. It is clearer in the Greek that, as an active commitment of one's life to God, faith has an intellectual component—the assent to teachings—that invariably leads to an entire way of life. In Hebrews, faith is described as "the assurance of things hoped for, the conviction of things not seen" (Heb. 11:1). Hebrews 11 describes the ways in which persons in the Old Testament trusted God, were used by God, and accomplished great things for God in the world. In the following chapter, Christ is called "the pioneer and perfecter of our faith," and the next part of the Epistle exhorts its readers to live faithfully in the world.

Faith, then, is much more than mental assent or a superficial prayer of commitment. It involves a radical trust of the whole person in God and a commitment of one's whole life to loving God and to loving all whom God loves. Rudolf Bultmann's article in *The Theological Dictionary of the New Testament* notes that early Christian usage of *pistis*, the Greek word for faith, involves belief in the truth of the message, obedience, trust, hope, and faithfulness.[5] Bultmann calls attention to Romans 10:9, where Paul says, "If you confess with your lips that Jesus is Lord and believe in your heart that God raised him from the dead, you will be saved." The words "confess with your lips" and "believe in your heart" form a synonymous parallelism. This suggests that there is an inner unity among the content of the faith, obedience to the will of God, hope in God's promises for the future, trusting one's life to God, and a personal relationship with Jesus as Lord.

One of Paul's arguments in Romans, Galatians, and Ephesians centers on the way in which salvation in Christ comes through faith rather than works of the law. Faith in this case is a positive response to the relationship God offers us in Christ. That response marks the beginning of the transformation of our minds and hearts. We are changed so that we become more obedient to the law. While some in apostolic times—and throughout Christian history as well—have misinterpreted Paul's teaching to be antinomian, he teaches that faith and the law are both important. He says, "Do we then overthrow the law by this faith? By no means! On the contrary, we uphold the law" (Rom. 3:31). In fact, the structure of many of Paul's writings takes the form of stressing the grace of God; human acceptance of a new, transforming relationship through faith; and the way in which faithful persons then live out the requirements of the law. As early as the second century, Christian exegesis came to understand that it was not the ceremonial parts of the law that were binding, but its moral parts.[6] Similarly, the Gospel of Matthew is often misunderstood. Matthew 28:19-20 is quoted as if making disciples was only helping people enter the Christian life. Here Jesus says, "[teach] them to obey everything I have commanded you." As a summary of the whole Gospel, this verse refers to obeying all of the commandments in the previous chapters. Matthew has in mind Jesus' call to a radical, costly discipleship.

Love as Response to the Reign of God

For both exegetical and logical reasons, God's love is an illuminating starting point for a theology of evangelism. God loves the world enough to send the Son to save humanity. The election of Israel, the word of the Lord given to the prophets, and the sending of the Son are the major divine initiatives to fulfill God's reign among humanity and the rest of creation.

The appropriate human response to the reign of God is obedience to God's will. Of all the commands in the Old Testament, Jesus gives two the highest priority. In addition, he links up these commands with the presence of the reign of God. In Matthew's version he goes beyond prioritization to say that everything else in God's will hangs on these two commands. The text is familiar, but its importance requires careful study.

> One of the scribes came near and heard them disputing with one another, and seeing that he answered them well, he asked him, "Which commandment is the first of all?" Jesus answered, "The first is, 'Hear, O Israel: the Lord our God, the Lord is one; you shall love the Lord your God with all your heart, and with all your soul, and with all your mind, and with all your strength.' The second is this, 'You shall love your neighbor as yourself.' There is no other commandment greater than these." Then the scribe said to him, "You are right, Teacher; you have truly said that 'he is one, and besides him there is no other'; and 'to love him with all the heart, and with all the understanding, and with all the strength,' and 'to love one's neighbor as oneself,'—this is much more important than all whole burnt offerings and sacrifices." When Jesus saw that he answered wisely, he said to him, "You are not far from the kingdom of God." (Mark 12:28-34)[7]

Matthew's version is similar, but instead of "there is no other commandment greater than these," Jesus says, "On these two commandments hang all the law and the prophets" (Matt. 22:40). Luke's version does not focus explicitly on exegesis of the commandments. Rather, the question put to him by the lawyer is, "what must I do to inherit eternal life?" It is the lawyer who names the two commandments, and Jesus replies, "You have given the right answer; do this and you will live" (Luke 10:28). This is followed by the parable of the good Samaritan, which is itself precipitated by the lawyer's question "who is my neighbor?"

What can be said about all three of these versions considered together? While each of the Gospels has a slightly different portrayal of the questioners, all of the episodes involve dialogue with religious leaders about the central matters of relationship with God. In Matthew and Luke the questioner is a lawyer, who is best understood as a professional theologian.[8] This is a discussion about how best to interpret the commandments in the Old Testament and thereby find the right way to live. In Mark, the questioner is a scribe.

In each case, Jesus quotes Deuteronomy 6:5 as the first and greatest commandment. In Mark he gives the opening affirmation of God's oneness as well. While it is not clear why Matthew and Luke do not include this, affirmation of Deuteronomy 6:4 would have been brought to mind by the citation of verse 5. Thus, Jesus begins with the oneness of God, which Eugene Boring describes as "the closest thing to a universal creed in Judaism."[9] Jesus then combines it with the love of neighbor from Leviticus 19, a combination which Boring says is "distinctive of the synoptic Jesus," even though it also appears in later Hellenistic Jewish writings.[10]

More important, Matthew's version has Jesus say that all of the law and the prophets "hang" on these two texts. It is important to remember that in Jesus' time, the "law and the prophets" were the entirety of the Jewish Scriptures, since the writings had not yet been canonized. In Mark, Jesus says that these two commandments are more important than the sacrificial system of worship. For Luke, they are the key to eternal life.

Taking all three Gospel versions together, loving God with everything one has and loving one's neighbor as oneself has a kind of priority and centrality to God's will for humanity that is of the highest order. All other duties flow from and are subordinate to these two commands. Since "love" is a relational word, this involves the kind of response that the rest of the New Testament describes as faith. Human beings are called by God to give themselves totally to God. In so doing, they are to love all those whom God loves. Called "the neighbor" in the Leviticus text, the other whom we are to love is an all-inclusive other. The parable of the good Samaritan delineates a despised category of persons as the neighbor.

The commandment to love is linked with how one should respond to the coming reign of God. In Mark, the conversation with the scribe is friendly, and Jesus agrees with the scribe's answer. Because he understood the importance of loving God and neighbor, Jesus told him that he was not far from the reign of God. For the lawyer in Luke's Gospel, receiving eternal life is equivalent to entering the reign of God.[11] While Matthew's question is posed in a more exegetical form, the connection with other versions of the love command makes it clear that in the reign of God, love is supreme.

The centrality of the Great Commandments is borne out in much of the rest of Jesus' teaching. In Matthew 5:44-45 Jesus taught that persons should love their enemies and pray for their persecutors, "so that you may be children of your Father in heaven." Jesus is clear that the neighbor includes everyone, even Samaritans and enemies. In John's Gospel and the associated epistles, the love commandment takes a different form. One abides in Christ's love and is thereby enabled to love others as the branches partake of the vine (John 13:34, 15:12, 17). In John 15:17, while it is apparent that the new community is to love one another, the tie between loving Christ and keeping his commandments is explicit (see John 14:15).

Given the predominance of these commandments to love others, several other texts can be interpreted as specifications of what love requires in different situations. Matthew 25:31-46 teaches that feeding the hungry, giving drink to the thirsty, welcoming the stranger, and clothing the naked are all essential to entering the reign of God, which is also called eternal life. Zacchaeus's restoration of money to those he had defrauded and his distribution of his wealth to the poor is an instance of a loving response to the reign of God. The money changers' defiling the temple with their transactions is a failure to love God fully. Similarly, it will be argued below that the command to make disciples and to bear witness is also a manifestation of the primary command to love others.

The Great Commandments, then, are a helpful way to organize and interpret the rest of Scripture with regard to how human beings are to respond to God's grace. Loving God is tied to entry into eternal life. It summarizes the prophets' concern with justice for the poor, the widows, and the orphans. It summarizes their concern with right relationship to God and proper worship. It is the foundation on which Paul's theology is built. To respond to the reign of God is to receive God's grace and to follow the Great Commandments.

God's Mission and the Mission of the Church

The God who is love is a missionary God who seeks to save the world. God's loving reign as sovereign over the creation aims at justice, peace, and love. Given the state of human sin, this requires judgment and reconciliation, both between God and humanity and within the human community. God's election of Israel is a key turning point in the history of salvation. God chose Abraham to be in a special relationship with God. Because of Abraham's faithfulness, all the nations of the earth would be blessed (Gen. 12:2-3).

God's mission to the world, sometimes referred to by the Latin words *missio Dei*, refers to the divine activity of redeeming the world from sin and accomplishing God's purposes. Preeminently, it refers to the sending of the Son into the world to be born, live, and die as Jesus of Nazareth. After Christ's time on earth, the Holy Spirit was sent into the world to fulfill all the functions that were promised the disciples.[12] For these reasons, mission is first and foremost an activity of God in the world.[13]

How then do we understand the mission of the church? It is crucial that one begin with God's mission and see that God has called the church into being and created it to participate in it. Carlos Cardoza-Orlandi defines mission as "the participation of the people of God in God's action in the world."[14] God's action is more extensive than the work of the church. God is at work using other means to accomplish the *missio Dei*. Isaiah believed that God used Cyrus and he called the Persian ruler "Messiah." God is using all the resources at God's disposal. Thus, Cardoza-Orlandi says, the church is called "to discern God's action in the world and to participate in God's mission."[15]

Nevertheless, the church is a privileged part of this *missio Dei*. The church is entrusted with the fullness of God's self-disclosure. It is in the church that authentic worship takes place. God's will is followed in many different ways and God's grace is active outside the church and its ministry. But the church remains the best way for humans to participate in the reign of God precisely because it embodies that reign in a visible way. It is the Body of Christ.

One of the problems with this characterization is that sometimes the church fails to be the church. Its worship is impoverished. It preaches another gospel than the one "that was once for all entrusted to the saints" (Jude 3). It succumbs to the sins of the world rather than pointing to the righteousness of God. One of the most significant ways in which the church fails to be the church is when it becomes a club for the benefit of its own members. Cardoza-Orlandi quotes Emil Brunner as saying, "Mission is to the church what combustion is to fire," and draws the conclusion that there is no church without mission.[16] Yet, we have experiences with Christian bodies where the sense of participating in God's mission no longer exists. These bodies have adopted various forms of inwardness, institutional maintenance, or self-centeredness and no longer strive to discern how they can best be used by God for the larger mission God has in mind. William J. Abraham responds to this phenomenon in a graphic way. He said something like the following in a speech to United Methodist leaders, "God is at work saving the world. God is going to accomplish God's purposes. That is certain. The only interesting question is whether God will find the United Methodist Church a fit instrument to use in this activity, or whether God will give up on us and find someone else to use." [17]

While there is no single word for "mission" in the New Testament,[18] the idea of mission is so embedded in the text that it is best described as a missionary document. By this I do not mean that it was written to non-Christian people as a tool for the missionaries to use. Rather, it was written by missionaries to missionaries as part of the life of the first-century church. David Bosch proposes, along with Martin Hengel, "that the history and theology of early Christianity are, first of all, 'mission history' and 'mission theology.'"[19] He continues, "the New Testament authors were less interested in definitions of mission than in the missionary existence of their readers; to give expression to the latter they used a rich variety of metaphors, such as 'the salt of the earth,' 'the light of the world,' 'a city on a hill,' and the like."[20] Christianity is intrinsically missionary. It exists to worship God and serve God's mission to the world. It best serves God's mission by bearing witness to what God has done, is doing, and will do.

It is possible to describe Christian existence as composed of these two tasks: worship that is centered on God and bearing witness that is centered on others. But there is an intermediate step whereby the church itself must attend to its own formation as a fit instrument to participate in God's mission. Thus a threefold formula of the church's task—worship, formation, and witness—corresponds to the three objects Christians are called to love in the Great Commandments. By worship we love God. By formation we love ourselves. By witness we love others. This threefold approach illuminates how the church responds to the reign of God in obedience to God's commands. However, the three categories are not discrete. One important clue is found in Romans 12:1 where Paul appeals to the reader "to present your bodies as a living sacrifice, holy and acceptable to God which is your spiritual worship." This is tied in with having one's life transformed by the renewing of the mind. What follows in chapter 12 is a discussion of the various ways in which Christians are called, among other things, to bear witness using spiritual gifts to build up others, to love, to hate evil, to rejoice, to suffer patiently, to pray perseveringly, to contribute to the needs of the saints, and to extend hospitality.

When the church is the church, the worship it offers God is spiritually formative. It shapes the lives of the worshipers. Similarly, worship in which the gospel is preached and read leads to bearing witness in the world. True spiritual formation creates a loving character that both motivates persons to bear witness and helps them persevere in it. Success and failure in bearing witness drives the believer back to worship to thank God for what has been accomplished by God's grace and to confess one's failures in the assigned tasks.

The Christian life is a multifaceted relationship between the church and God that shapes the lives of the believers. When they give to God and others, they receive. Thus, in the discussion that follows, it can be seen that one activity has many different aspects.

Humanity's Response as Worship

Humanity's first response should be to love God with all one's heart, soul, mind, and strength (Mark 12:30). Leander Keck in his *Church Confident* proposes that renewing any institution requires revitalizing its core, its reason for being. Unless this core is refocused and funded afresh, renewal becomes a matter of strategy for survival. Accordingly, the churches' renewal becomes possible only when their religious vitality is energized again by a basic reform of their worship of God. Worship enacts and proclaims a construal of Reality and our relation to it. Aidan Kavanagh put it well: In liturgy the church "is caught in the act of being most overtly itself as it stands faithfully in the presence of the One who is both the object and the source of . . . faith." [21]

The worship of God is the main task of the church on which all else depends. While Keck's book is focused on church renewal, the centrality of worship for the life of the community is evident in his argument. The gathering of the community to praise God, give thanks to God, hear God's word read and proclaimed, and participate in the sacraments is essential to Christian life.

One of the earliest responses to the risen Lord was worship (Matt. 28:17). It is presumed throughout the New Testament that Christians will pray. Jesus said to his disciples, "When you are praying" (Matt. 6:7), assuming they would do so. After Pentecost, the Christian community "devoted themselves to the apostles' teaching and fellowship, to the breaking of bread and the prayers" (Acts 2:42).

Paul's exhortation "to present your bodies as a living sacrifice, holy and acceptable to God, which is your spiritual worship" (Rom. 12:1) indicates that the worship of God has a strong connection with the ways in which Christians live in the world. All of life is to be seen as worship in the deepest sense of the word, and the gathering of the Christian community on Sundays is simply one form that it takes. In the same way, formal prayers, whether corporate, family, or individual should simply focus the kind of prayer that one does without ceasing (1 Thess. 5:17). Fulfilling Paul's command in 1 Thessalonians is impossible unless praying is seen as a quality of life in which all of one's activities—work, school, leisure, service—are devoted to God. This quality of life where all of one's time is lived in the awareness of God's presence gets focused in corporate worship where we explicitly acknowledge God's presence and seek to communicate with God.

Humanity's Response as Formation

Because of the intrinsic relation between the two Great Commandments, worshiping God is the first step in loving oneself. To become truly and fully human we must love God and be in the right relationship to God. Augustine said it well in the *Confessions*: "for thou has made us for thyself and restless is our heart until it comes to rest in thee."[22]

Thus, part of the mission of each human being who responds to God's grace with faith is to attend to one's own spiritual formation so that one becomes the person God has called one to be. This means learning to love God better with one's mind—growing intellectually. This means learning to love God better with one's heart—growing emotionally. This means learning to love God better with one's behavior—growing morally.

Marjorie Thompson presents an integrated understanding of spiritual formation. She prefers the term "the spiritual life." She says, "Scripturally speaking, the spiritual life is simply the increasing vitality and sway of God's Spirit in us. It is a magnificent choreography of the Holy Spirit in the human spirit, moving us toward communion with both Creator and creation. It has to do with God's way of relating to us, and our way of responding to God."[23]

There could easily be a deep misunderstanding of my saying that one of the Christian's obligations is to love oneself. In a materialistic and hedonistic culture like twenty-first-century America, such a claim is easily misinterpreted as a self-centered advocacy of personal fulfillment by accumulating more things or experiences. Instead, the kind of love the gospel calls for us to have is the fulfillment that comes from being in a right relationship with God. By giving ourselves to God and others, we find the deepest happiness and abundant life. Loving oneself is not wrong. Loving oneself in the way that a sinful world advises one to love is a mistake of the greatest significance.

Humanity's Response as Bearing Witness

The fulfillment of humanity's duty to love others can be described as bearing witness. While the adequacy of this overall category may be disputed, it has the advantage of integrating several different facets into a single whole. The verbal action of speaking the truth as it is in Jesus—whether that truth is about God, Christ, the way of salvation, or God's demand for justice—is integrated with actions that point toward the love of God for the world and God's demand that the world cease its evil ways and learn genuine peace. All of these activities are ways in which Christians bear witness to the love of God. Micah 6:8 says, "He has told you, O mortal, what is good; and what does the LORD require of you but to do justice, and to love kindness, and to walk humbly with your God?" All of these are ways of bearing witness, and the impact of words and deeds together makes for a stronger witness than either one separately. Persons who are inclined more toward one or the other often undervalue the ways in which deeds are misunderstood without verbal witness and the ways in which words are thought cheap without deeds to match.

In addition, the characterization of humanity's love for others as bearing witness is the foundation of Christ's command in Acts 1:8. Christ says, "But you will receive power when the Holy Spirit has come upon you; and you will be my witnesses in Jerusalem, in all Judea and Samaria, and to the ends of the earth."

The category of being witnesses for Christ also has the advantage in that it deals with whole persons. Far too often only one aspect of a person is considered in the ministry of the church. Persons are sometimes regarded as souls that need to be given an insurance policy for life after death. This ignores the need for food or clothing, and treats persons as bodiless souls. At other times persons are regarded as materialistic creatures, and justice is construed as equality of wealth. This treats persons as soulless bodies.

An adequate theological anthropology will look at human beings as complex creatures with many different needs. The love of God seeks to meet all of those needs in a holistic way. Persons have physical needs for food, water, clothing, and shelter. When they are ill, they need healing. They also need communities. Persons need moral values to show them how best to live in loving and nurturing communities.[24] Persons need protection from the evil of others. Persons need systems of punishment and justice to maintain protection for the weak and to provide opportunities for rehabilitation for the guilty. Persons need forgiveness when they have sinned, and reconciliation with God and neighbor for the actions that cause separation and estrangement. Persons also need to be in right relationship with God, and so they need to be evangelized.

EVANGELISM IS AN INTEGRAL PART OF MISSION

From all that has been said here, the relationship between evangelism and mission is made visible. Bosch says, "Mission includes *evangelism* as one of its essential dimensions."[25] Yet, mission is wider than evangelism. Bosch quotes Moltmann, who says, "Evangelization is mission but mission is not merely evangelization."[26] Dana Robert uses the heart-body metaphor, saying,

> The relationship of evangelism to mission is like the relationship of the heart to the body. Mission is the body. It walks and moves in different contexts. Sometimes the hands are busy and sometimes the feet. Sometimes the eyes are ineffective because the night is so dark that they are useless, and the hands are needed to feel the way. But always the heart beats, sending the blood through the body, nourishing the other organs and keeping the body alive. Evangelism is the heart, both as the pump that circulates the life force and as the seat of the emotions. Without the emotional fervor of the heart, the love affair with the gospel, mission dies. To separate the heart from the body is to kill the body. To take evangelism out of mission is to cut the heart out of it.[27]

Conversely, she notes that the two concepts should not be conflated, saying

> To merge the two concepts so that evangelism and mission are the same thing has historically led some evangelicals to drop emphasis on the reign of God so that anything beyond verbal proclamation is not mission. On the other hand, in the 1970s it was popular for some ecumenical Christians to argue that everything the church does is evangelism since it flows from Christian motivation, even if the Good News of Jesus Christ is never mentioned. With evangelism as the heart of Christian mission, however, one can neither separate the two nor rank forms of mission into a formulaic hierarchy of priorities.[28]

The heart-body metaphor is helpful in showing how essential and central evangelism is to the mission of the church. Robert is right;

if you cut out the heart the body dies. The limit of the metaphor, however, is that the heart only serves the body and never does the things that impact the world outside of the body directly. Misusing this metaphor, one might conclude that evangelism—the gospel—is the motivation for Christian mission in the world, but that Christian mission is never evangelism. While I do not believe that is Robert's intended point, the limits of the metaphor should be delineated.

It would be better to speak about evangelism as one of the constitutive aspects of mission. An analogy with the complexity of parenting may be helpful here. In raising a child, good parents have multiple goals. The relationship is complex. It should be motivated and guided by love. Christian parents seek to raise a child that is virtuous, well-educated, and Christian, among other things. One does not *make* a child any of these things. Rather, in the course of a multiyear relationship, one takes various actions that serve all of these goals. In every case external circumstances and the free choices of the child will affect the outcome. But the parent's intentions are clear. Sometimes, one action will aim at all of the goals, such as sending a child on a mission trip to a different country. Other times, one pursues the goals one at a time. Yet these multiple intentions form a coherent whole—the goal of raising children to be mature, well-educated, and virtuous Christians.

In the same way, our response to the reign of God takes place in the midst of God's plan for the world. The task of pursuing that plan is the *missio Dei,* and the church shares in it by pursuing its mission. Evangelism is one part of the plan. There are other parts as well.

The reminder that evangelism has a great deal to do with matters of politics, social justice, and economics is a fundamental contribution of those Latin American liberation theologians that have written about evangelism. Priscilla Pope-Levison, in a study of ten such persons as well as documents from both Roman Catholic and World Council of Churches sources, concludes, "Evangelization is being incorporated into liberating the oppressed, instigating structural change, and working for God's reign."[29] She regards this as a holistic, comprehensive trend that will help shape the thinking of both Protestants and Roman Catholics in years to come.

This liberation perspective should help shape our understanding of what it means to love persons well. It applies the tools of social, economic, and political analysis to ask how we can fulfill God's commandment to love the poor and the marginalized. It seeks to discern where the Holy Spirit is moving in the world today with the most sophisticated methods developed by the human mind, but always in the light of Scripture.

Mission and Hospitality

The paradox of two opposite movements characterizes the identity of the church at a fundamental level. On the one hand, the church is a holy people, set apart by the call of God and ordained to a special identity in the world. First Peter 2:9-11 captures this aspect of the church's calling as follows:

> But you are a chosen race, a royal priesthood, a holy nation, God's own people, in order that you may proclaim the mighty acts of him who called you out of darkness into his marvelous light. Once you were not a people, but now you are God's people; once you had not received mercy, but now you have received mercy. Beloved, I urge you as aliens and exiles to abstain from the desires of the flesh that wage war against the soul.

Here the church, a unique people that were not previously a people, is given the role of serving God's mission to the world. Such a mission inevitably sets them off from others who are outsiders. They are to be separate, to live as aliens and exiles. In the words of the KJV, they are to be a "peculiar people."

At the same time, the New Testament frequently urges hospitality to the stranger. Hebrews says, "Let mutual love continue. Do not neglect to show hospitality to strangers, for by doing that some have entertained angels without knowing it" (Heb. 13:1-2).[30] The very success of the mission, which 1 Peter claims and which is fundamental to Christian identity, requires that the community practice a level of hospitality that makes love genuine.

The church's missionary nature holds both holiness and hospitality in tension. Walter Klaiber speaks of the missionary nature of the congregation that must not conform to the world, but must have a creative nonconformity which lets the alternative possibility for living which grows out of the gospel become visible to the outside world. A missionary congregation will, therefore, have to find its way between an "opening" of the house of God which is so all-encompassing that neither contours nor functions of this house are still recognizable, because the protective roof and the walls which encompass it have been taken away for the sake of openness on the one side, and on the other there has been a shutting-out of the outside world so that the missionary activities appear more like short-term skirmishes outside the fortress under siege than like an invitation to enter through open doors.[31]

Then, he offers an unforgettable metaphor:

The church of Jesus Christ lives in gathering and scattering, in being called together and in being sent forth. This dual motion is as necessary for her life as breathing in and breathing out is for human life. Wherever one or the other atrophies, the local church becomes ill and dies away. To put it a bit bluntly: A congregation which lives only for its own in-gathering and self-nurture will die of spiritual arteriosclerosis; a congregation which pursues an unmitigated activism of missionary and service programs will succumb to consumption.[32]

Mission, therefore, is a combination of bringing people together and nurturing their identity as a separated people on the one hand, and sending them out to serve God in all that they do on the other hand. The mission statement of the United Methodist Church is "to make disciples of Jesus Christ." It goes on to explain how this is done:

We make disciples as we:

—proclaim the gospel, seek, welcome and gather persons into the body of Christ;

—lead persons to commit their lives to God through baptism and profession of faith in Jesus Christ;

—nurture persons in Christian living through worship, the sacraments, spiritual disciplines, and other means of grace, such as Wesley's Christian conferencing;

—send persons into the world to live lovingly and justly as servants of Christ by healing the sick, feeding the hungry, caring for the stranger, freeing the oppressed, and working to develop social structures that are consistent with the gospel; and

—continue the mission of seeking, welcoming and gathering persons into the community of the body of Christ.[33]

This process of reaching new persons with the gospel, helping them connect with God's grace, and then facilitating their going out to live "lovingly and justly" as disciples in the world describes the same sort of breathing in and breathing out for which Klaiber calls.

CHAPTER THREE

The Logic of Discipleship

To respond in conscious faith to an encounter with the reign of God is to become a disciple of Jesus Christ. Disciples seek to live obediently to God's will, participating in God's mission according to the best of their abilities and appropriately for their contexts. Throughout this book I argue that evangelism is best understood as an aspect of the church's mission that seeks to help persons enter into Christian discipleship. An essential part of this argument is a discussion of the logic of discipleship.

Evaluating *The Logic of Evangelism*

William J. Abraham's 1989 book *The Logic of Evangelism* gives an extended critique of positions that understand evangelism as proclamation or church growth. His analyses of these positions will be considered in the next chapter, but they are well-founded. He argues that both proclamation and church growth are parts of evangelism, but they are inadequate characterizations of the whole ministry of evangelism. More briefly, he notes three other conceptions of evangelism and suggests that they only partially describe what evangelism is all about. The first two of these are converting persons to Christianity and sharing testimonies of what God has done.[1] The last conception he considers focuses on discipleship. He says:

> Lamenting the gross inadequacy of recording decisions without any serious follow-up and instruction, some have insisted that the essence of evangelism lies in making disciples who are not only brought to a decision to follow Christ but are also taught to be disciples. The young disciple is instructed in the fundamentals of faith and piety, with the goal of being the kind of person who can make disciples of others.[2]

Abraham then concludes, "These three ways [conversion, testimony, and discipleship] grow naturally out of the coming of the rule of God on earth."[3]

Abraham's Main Thesis

Abraham's extended analysis of evangelism as church growth and proclamation and his brief discussion of the other three models lay the foundation for his primary thesis. Although he argues that these are all important dimensions of the coming rule of God, he says that none of them represents the essence of evangelism. He then proposes his own definition as follows: "We can best improve our thinking on evangelism by conceiving it as that set of intentional activities which is governed by the goal of initiating people into the kingdom of God for the first time."[4]

Abraham's most significant contribution to the theology of evangelism is his focus on the concept of initiation in its broad sense. Acknowledging that there are other, more narrow senses of the word, he suggests that initiation "is an act or set of acts that admits one into a society, a set of principles, a body of knowledge, a way of living, and the like. . . . To initiate someone into the kingdom of God is to admit that person into the eschatological rule of God through appropriate instruction, experiences, rites and forms."[5]

This is a brilliant insight that at once connects and shows the relationships among all of the competing definitions of evangelism. Each of them is a partial understanding of a complex process. By focusing on evangelism as initiation, Abraham can then suggest that there are many different activities that all contribute to that complex activity. This is the reason that Abraham uses "intention."

By relying on the intention of the evangelist, Abraham can distinguish between activities that are genuinely evangelistic and those that are not. The criterion is what the evangelist aims to do. Proclamation can aim at initiation into the reign of God, or it can aim at something else entirely. Christian preaching sometimes proclaims God's word with the goal of helping persons who are already Christians grow toward spiritual maturity. It can aim at bringing about obedience on a particular issue. But where proclamation aims at initiation of persons, it is evangelistic.

Similarly, the use of "intention" allows for a wider range of actions to be construed as evangelistic. Feeding hungry persons can be evangelistic, as can advocating for social justice in a community. In both cases, there may be multiple intentions at work in the same action, because the agents know that by feeding hungry persons they are demonstrating God's love in ways that will invite persons to respond faithfully. Thus, one action can have multiple effects and intentionally so. In this way, as we will show in the next chapter, the phrase "intentional activities governed by the goal of initiating persons" provides exactly the flexibility that a workable theology of evangelism needs.

Abraham makes the further point "that the activity or experience or institution into which one is initiated determines the material character of the initiation under review."[6] Initiation into the kingdom of God will have its own unique logic and grammar and will require its own agenda.[7] Initiation into the kingdom will not be like initiation into anything else. It shifts the focus away from what human beings do in certain ceremonies and catechesis. Instead,

> our eyes are fixed on what God has done in Christ, and on what the Holy Spirit continues to do now. We shift from an anthropocentric horizon, where the focus is on what we do or on what is done to us in certain rites and ceremonies, in various acts of catechesis and the like; we move from this to a theocentric horizon where the focus is on the majestic and awesome activity of a trinitarian God whose actions on our behalf stagger our imagination and dissolve into impenetrable mystery. It is extraordinarily difficult to capture this conceptually and even more demanding to sustain it across the generations, but in itself this shift of horizon should radically alter the whole temper and ethos of our evangelistic ministries. I can think of nothing more important or more decisive in charting the contours of a healthy vision of evangelism than this shift of focus.[8]

Six Aspects of Initiation

The focus on the kingdom of God is Abraham's starting point, and the idea of initiation unites many disparate understandings of evangelism into one inclusive definition. As his argument progresses, he suggests that there are six aspects of initiation into the kingdom. When they are first mentioned Abraham observes that each one alone is insufficient. He says,

> Evangelism, too, is intimately related to the sweep of God's action in history. It arises out of the inauguration of God's sovereign rule on earth, and its central aim is to see people firmly grounded within that rule so that they can begin a new life as agents of reconciliation, compassion, and peace. Its unique and irreplaceable role in the life of the church is to initiate people into the dynamic rule of God that was ontologically grounded in the work of Jesus Christ in Israel and is continued and sustained by grace through the inimitable activity of the Holy Spirit. Such initiation is *sui generis*. It cannot be collapsed into admittance to some religious institution. It is logically distinct from the kind of psychological and social formation that takes place when one embraces a specific cosmic or historical narrative. It cannot be reduced to the acquisition of some kind of creed or body of knowledge that is intellectually mastered, and it is more than the appropriation of a particular moral vision. It is distinct from the passive endurance of certain rites and ceremonies, it goes far beyond the undergoing of some spiritual or emotional experiences of even the most positive character, and it cannot be drained out into an assiduous activism that seeks to change the world for the better. To be initiated into the rule of God is to encounter a transcendent reality that has entered human history and to find oneself drawn up into the ultimate purposes of God for history and creation. Initiation involves most if not all of the processes we have just identified, yet to reduce it to any or all of them is to foment theological folly and spiritual confusion.[9]

He then says:

> Initiation involves a complex web of reality that is at once corporate, cognitive, moral, experiential, operational and disciplinary. Initiation into the kingdom of God is not only one of these; nor is it all of these strung together as a mere human enterprise driven

simply by earthly passion and planning; it is all of these set and bounded within the dramatic action of God that is manifest in Christ and fueled by the Holy Spirit.[10]

Abraham's proposal does two very important things. First, it preserves the significance of the reign of God in God's mission to the world. This important aspect of Jesus' preaching is central to Abraham's understanding of evangelism. Second, it recognizes that evangelism is a polymorphous activity that can take a variety of forms. If one says, "This afternoon I am going out to do some evangelism," there are many different activities that could fulfill such an intention. I will argue in the appendix that a comprehensive system of evangelism based in a congregation must include many different activities.

William Abraham clarifies that there are four agents involved in evangelism. He says, "The primary agent is the triune God who has created us in his own image, who has acted decisively in Jesus of Nazareth for the liberation of the cosmos, and who has come in the person of the Holy Spirit to make known the work of Christ and to empower God's people to live as his disciples and to participate in his activity in the world."[11] Abraham then notes that the church, the evangelist, and the person or persons being evangelized are also agents who participate in the process. He concludes, "Evangelism, therefore, calls for the activity of multiple agents; it is never a solo performance. Even when the evangelist may appear to be acting alone, his or her activity depends on the concomitant activity of the Holy Spirit."[12]

This is an important reminder for persons who think of evangelism as a purely human activity. It is important to remember that the initiative in saving the world lies with God. It is the love of God that initiates God's mission, and whatever part human beings play in that mission has the character of participation in something larger than themselves.

It is precisely this that is troubling in Abraham's proposal. By focusing on initiation into the reign of God and by requiring the church and the evangelist to be agents who are active, however subordinately in the process, Abraham has in fact limited the extent of God's reign to the reach of the church. According to Abraham's definition, persons can be initiated into the reign of God only when the church is involved as an agent. This interpretation of

Abraham's position is supported by his view of the six aspects of initiation. One of them, baptism, requires the sacramental initiation into the Body of Christ as part of entering the reign of God. Another one, the intellectual understanding and commitment to the doctrines taught in the creeds of the church also ties initiation into the reign of God with the church's doctrine. The other four aspects—morality, conversion, spiritual gifts, and disciplines—could conceivably be interpreted in ways that would not require the presence or ministry of the church.

Thus, Abraham's proposal makes the reign of God no wider than the ministry of the church. Initiation into the reign of God cannot take place without the agency of the church, without the sacrament of baptism into the church, and without accepting the church's doctrine. This does not amount to the reign of God being coextensive with the church. It is possible that, based on Abraham's position, one could argue that the reign of God is actually smaller than the visible church. But Abraham's position does commit him to the reign of God not being larger than the visible church. Where there is no church, there can be no reign of God.

In an essay published ten years after *The Logic of Evangelism*, Abraham has revised his position. In his earlier work he had wrestled with a dilemma of choosing between emphasizing initiation into the church or into the kingdom, and he had thought that the kingdom was both temporally and logically prior to the church.[13] His new position suggests, "What we need here is not a choice between the church and the kingdom, but a position which holds that both of these must be taken into consideration at once, and that when we do so we find that they complement each other in a deep way."[14] He offers four reasons for this new position. First, he says that initiating persons into the church and initiating them into the kingdom will involve the same issues. The larger context of his essay suggests that the ministry of making disciples of Jesus Christ is one of the marks of the church, and he appears to equate disciple-making with initiating persons into the church.[15] Second, he suggests that the tension between ecclesiology and eschatology is bogus.

> While formally it is right to insist on a logical distinction between the church and the kingdom, contingently and in reality, there is no kingdom without a community, the church, and there is no church without the presence of the kingdom. God's reign has

always had an Israel, an ecclesia, in history; it is not some sort of ahistorical, asocial reality. Equally the church would never have existed without the prior presence of the kingdom in history—in Israel, in Jesus Christ, and in Pentecost.[16]

Third, the distinction between church and kingdom is sometimes employed because of the failures and unfaithfulness of the church. These are realities that need to be accounted for, but one should focus "less on the wayward empirical realities of the church and more on a normative theological appraisal of her task and mission."[17] Last, treating the church as only one dimension of entry into the kingdom underplays its role in the work of making disciples.

Abraham then concludes:

> The primary task which *the church sets itself in making members is to initiate people into the kingdom of God* which has arrived in Jesus Christ through the working of the Holy Spirit. While the church through baptism and catechesis increases its membership, the work of the church in initiation is to point away from itself to a greater and more primordial reality, the kingdom of God.

He then discusses the failure of the church and proposes the following:

> The solution is to recognize that the problem is ecclesiological: failure to focus on the kingdom is precisely a failure in ecclesiology. It is to ignore the fact that the church exists in and for service to the kingdom out of which it originated. It is the church which is commissioned by the risen Lord to make disciples who will be initiated into the glorious reality of God's reign on earth, a reality that is fully incarnate in Jesus Christ and made available through the work of the Holy Spirit. If it does not do this it is simply failing to be the church.[18]

Abraham's modifications solve a number of crucial problems in the logic of his argument. It should be taken as a revision of his claim in 1989 that the model of disciple-making is an inadequate conception of evangelism.[19] Construing evangelism as initiation into Christian discipleship provides a logical foundation for his six aspects of initiation.

Abraham's more recent position is an improvement, but it still does not resolve the fundamental problem. By requiring the presence of the church for the existence of the reign of God, he has limited God's sovereign action on earth to be no larger than the ministry of the church. When he says, "there is no kingdom without a community, the church, and there is no church without the presence of the kingdom," he has unacceptably limited God's action to an institution that is partly human. God's sovereignty must be respected and the reality of God's gracious activity in establishing God's reign outside the church must be recognized.

This problem is best solved if one changes the focus of initiation. If we conceive of evangelism as initiation into Christian discipleship in response to the reign of God, we can avoid the conceptual problems inherent in both versions of Abraham's proposal. The additional advantage to this is that it provides a stronger foundation for deriving the various aspects of initiation.

My understanding of this new rationale involves something like the following: God is sovereign, and God is graciously reigning on earth in partial ways now. Further, God is bringing about the fulfillment of God's reign in the future. Human beings who encounter God's activity consciously and faithfully commit themselves to it. Christian discipleship includes the sacrament of baptism. Christian discipleship includes acceptance of the cognitive claims of Christian doctrine. Discipleship involves conversion, a new moral orientation, the reception of spiritual gifts, and the practice of spiritual disciplines. Locating these six as aspects of Christian discipleship rather than aspects of the reign of God allows one to argue why each one is necessary to discipleship. The debate about whether there ought to be six, more than six, or fewer than six aspects is a debate about how best to characterize Christian discipleship.

However, three crucial problems remain. First, the equation of the reign of God and the church is problematic. Second, there needs to be a seventh aspect. Third, there needs to be more emphasis on the congregational aspect of the church.

Ecclesiology and the Reign of God

Abraham's concern for the importance of the reign of God in evangelism can best be preserved if Christian discipleship is always discussed as the faithful response of persons to the reign of God. It is in fact God's love that is most important. God's mission to the world is an expression of God's love. God's mission aims at making persons disciples of Jesus Christ. Evangelism is that part of the church's mission that seeks to initiate persons into Christian discipleship in response to the reign of God. The whole majestic story of God's saving grace and God's self-giving in mission to the world is the essential context for any evangelistic activity by the church. The triune God is the primary agent in evangelism. Human agents play an important, but secondary role. The church's agency is, in part, the making of disciples. Abraham's new proposal makes this linkage explicit and clarifies an important point.

However, persons may well be initiated into the reign of God outside the ministry of the church. When Abraham claims that the kingdom must have the church, it entails the claim that when the church is not present the kingdom is not present. I would argue that the reign of God is most fully expressed in the church and that when persons fully encounter it and respond properly, the church comes into existence. But Abraham's new position preserves his previous limitation on where God's reign is active.

From a larger perspective, we do not want to limit the reign of God to the ministry of the church. It is God who is at work saving the world, and clearly God will use those persons and save those persons whom God chooses to use and save. Thus, whatever privileged position we understand the church to hold in God's mission, it is highly presumptuous to suppose that God is not at work outside the church. That view unacceptably limits God's saving activity to the church's ministry.

The same argument can be made for the activity of the evangelist. If a human evangelist is required for initiation into the reign of God, then the failure of humans to do evangelism limits the extent of the reign of God and the possibilities of entry into it. Such a limit restricts God's sovereign grace and God's ability to offer salvation to those God chooses to reach.

Abraham's argument for conceiving of evangelism as initiation is right. Further, his concern to relate evangelism to the action of God's reign coming into the world is right. The question is whether evangelism ought to be conceived as initiation into the reign of

God or not. Such a direct linkage causes a serious conceptual problem that ought to be avoided.

Addition of a Seventh Aspect

There is a seventh aspect of evangelism that should be included along with the other six. Jesus told the disciples to go and disciple others and that they would be his witnesses to the ends of the earth (Matt. 28:19, Acts 1:8). Any account of Christian discipleship, or any account of how Christians should respond to the reign of God, must include the missionary character of each Christian. They are called to bear witness to the world in a variety of ways.

Abraham's proposal could account for this aspect of discipleship under the category of morality. By construing all of morality under the category of bearing witness one could construct a category that includes evangelizing others and the varieties of ways that persons invite other persons into Christian discipleship. It is instructive, however, that in Abraham's discussion of the moral aspect of initiation, no mention is made of how Christians themselves have the responsibility of being active participants in the evangelistic process. While different persons will have different gifts and thus play different roles in the process, all Christians are expected to share their faith verbally with others. First Peter 3:15-16 is important here. It says, "Always be ready to make your defense to anyone who demands from you an accounting for the hope that is in you; yet do it with gentleness and reverence." Every Christian is to participate in faith-sharing as verbal witness to non-Christians. It does not require sophisticated apologetics. It does require the willingness and ability to tell someone else about one's relationship to God. Such testimonies are often more effective than sermons at inviting non-Christians to become disciples.

Given the current problems of many Protestant churches with encouraging Christians to share their faith with, invite and otherwise evangelize non-Christians, it is appropriate to make this emphasis explicit. The six categories should become seven. They are not discrete, as will be seen below; they overlap in significant ways.

Congregational Basis for Evangelism

Abraham's proposal needs improvement is another area. One needs to develop further his point that the church is one of the four key agents in the process of evangelism. Implicit in this claim is the absolutely crucial role played by congregations. By "congregation," I mean a gathered community of believers in which persons live the Christian life together. There the word of God is preached and the sacraments are duly administered.

Sometimes ecclesiology speaks of the church as the Body of Christ or as the community of the faithful or in other ways that are abstract. Such a large perspective is important, especially when speaking of baptism as incorporation into the Body of Christ or the unity of the church across space and time. But part of the attraction of Abraham's proposal is precisely its concreteness. Persons do not enter Christian discipleship because of some abstract entity called the church. They are not evangelized in any complete sense of the word by dioceses, conferences, mission agencies, or denominational structures. Rather, they are evangelized by individuals in communities of faith called congregations. Of the seven aspects, baptism, spiritual disciplines, and faith-sharing are best done by a congregation, or by individuals acting as representatives of a congregation. Baptism is best done by the congregation because it is a sacramental act of the community. In unusual circumstances persons are baptized without the congregation being present, such as the deathbed conversion and baptism of a person in a hospital. But most churches understand baptism as incorporation into the church in its concrete form as a congregation. So even if the sacrament does not take place while the community is gathered, the congregation is involved because the new believer has been added to its membership.

Spiritual disciplines are best nurtured in a congregation because worship is the most important discipline and it should involve a gathered community. Again, there are times when a person does not worship with the congregation for exceptional reasons such as being paralyzed and bedfast. In most circumstances, however, this part of discipleship is best done in a gathered community of faith. Part of discipleship is regular participation in the Eucharist practiced in community.

Again, faith-sharing is best done with a congregation because its goal is to initiate the non-Christian person into discipleship in a congregation. While one can think of exceptional circumstances, the normal course of events is for the new disciple to participate in the gathered community's life.

The other four—morality, conversion, spiritual gifts, and cognitive commitments—while possible in other settings, are also accomplished best in a congregation. Whatever the larger church does, it should do in order to support, encourage, require, or facilitate the evangelistic ministry of congregations.

At the other extreme, evangelism is sometimes conceived as something done primarily by individuals or parachurch organizations. The best of these recognize that initiation into Christian discipleship requires membership in a church, which requires participation in a congregation. They structure their evangelistic efforts to include a strong relationship with one or more congregations. At their worst, such efforts presume that, once a person has had a conversion experience, the evangelistic task is done and someone else can worry about discipleship. Or sometimes parachurch organizations presume that new converts only need to belong to their organization, thereby suggesting that their organization is all the church the person needs. Protestants in North America frequently have weak ecclesiologies, and the importance of the church in the Christian life is undervalued or ignored altogether.

Because evangelism is a polymorphous activity with three aspects that require a congregation, and four others that are best done by congregations, evangelism is most suited for congregations. Any deviation from this pattern runs the risk of truncating or fragmenting the evangelistic process.

Yet, because congregations often fail to exhibit their evangelistic character, there are important roles for judicatories and parachurch organizations in the ministry of evangelism. This works most powerfully when both of these groups understand their function as supplementing or supporting the work congregations ought to be doing themselves.

Three Steps of Discipleship with Seven Aspects

Standing as I do in the Wesleyan tradition, I believe that the way of salvation can best be summarized in three steps: repentance, justification, and sanctification. However, the outline of Christian discipleship offered here is not dependent on acceptance of a Wesleyan soteriology. Many Christian churches and many theologians would agree with this broad outline of soteriology, and many would say that it could be interpreted in a variety of ways. At the same time, modifications could be offered from various perspectives that would relate these three steps in ways that are different from what I have offered. The diversity within the Methodist tradition suggests that nuances are possible even within the framework of that tradition. In particular, there are different ways in which the seven aspects (baptism, cognitive commitments, spiritual disciplines, conversion, morality, spiritual gifts, and faith-sharing) might be arranged in relation to the three steps of repentance, justification, and sanctification.

I have argued elsewhere that the doctrine of salvation is central to the teaching of the United Methodist Church.[22] It was Wesley's contention and continues to be the contention of the United Methodist Church that their teaching should be construed as biblical Christianity. Neither Wesley nor United Methodism regards this body of teaching as solely Methodist. Rather it is viewed as the Methodist understanding of what all Christians should believe. This means United Methodists are deeply ecumenical. On the one hand, their teaching is open to correction from other Christians. On the other hand, their teaching is offered to the whole church as their understanding of what the Christian church should teach. I have proposed what I hope is recognizable as at least one plausible Christian understanding of discipleship. The view of discipleship described here uses a Wesleyan soteriology without requiring its acceptance. Because the definition of evangelism focuses on initiation into Christian discipleship, changes in the understanding of discipleship require corresponding changes in the theology of evangelism. For convenience and clarity of presentation, and because of the authority carried by Wesley in some denominations, quotations from Wesley will be used to explicate these three steps of Christian discipleship. James C. Logan suggests that a Wesleyan approach to evangelism might be a significant resource for the current discussion.

> The Wesleyan heritage in its earliest days possessed a grasp of the wholeness of the gospel as grace active in mission. In our time we have a plenitude of truncated gospels, inside the church and out.

A recovery of the trajectory of wholeness, both of grace and mission, could be a mighty corrective to current social accommodations of the gospel. Wesley's message was no superficial gospel catering to the whims of the moment. It was a whole gospel for persons, church and society.[23]

While the Wesleyan approach is only one of many possible ways of thinking about evangelism, it provides considerable advantages in articulating a holistic approach to the issues involved. In many cases similar resources from other Christian traditions could reinforce, correct, and supplement the approach offered here.

The beginning point of the way of salvation is humanity's creation in the image of God. The image of God, however, has been marred by the disease of sin. Called "prevenient" or "preventing" because it comes before our awareness of it, God's grace is offered to all human beings. God is continually wooing each person into a saving relationship with God. Salvation begins with God's grace awakening persons to their need of God and inviting them to respond. Even humanity's ability to respond is a gift of grace. This means all human goodness is ascribed to God's gracious, saving love.

Salvation is best understood as a process. Wesley says:

> If we take this in its utmost extent it will include all that is wrought in the soul by what is frequently termed "natural conscience," but more properly, "preventing grace"; all the "drawings" of "the Father," the desires after God, which, if we yield to them, increase more and more; all that "light" wherewith the Son of God "enlighteneth everyone that cometh into the world," showing every man "to do justly, to love mercy, and to walk humbly with his God"; all the convictions which his Spirit from time to time works in every child of man. Although it is true the generality of men stifle them as soon as possible, and after a while forget, or at least deny, that ever they had them at all. But we are at present concerned only with that salvation which the Apostle is directly speaking of. And this consists of two general parts, justification and sanctification.[24]

Thus, salvation is possible only by the grace of God.

In the past, too many evangelists have assumed that Christ is not present if Christ is not explicitly named. This is far too limiting. A doctrine of prevenient grace recognizes that God is at work in all situations, enlightening everyone (John 1:9).[25] The evangelist's first task, then, is to listen for indications of God's grace that are already present in the situation at the time of one's arrival.

Repentance

Repentance is the turning away from sin, evil, and other gods and toward the one true God. The biblical words *shub* and *epistrephein* carry connotations of turning. Another Greek word often used in the New Testament, *metanoia*, carries connotations of changing one's mind and heart. Repentance is evidenced by the sort of behavior that shows one is truly seeking to live in a new relationship with God and to obey God's will for one's life. Two key texts in the Gospels illustrate this sense of turning and changing one's ways. In the story of the prodigal son, the literary structure of the first half of the story points one to the central verse. In Luke 15:17-19 it says, "But when he came to himself he said, 'How many of my father's hired hands have bread enough and to spare, but here I am dying of hunger! I will get up and go to my father, and I will say to him, "Father, I have sinned against heaven and before you; I am no longer worthy to be called your son; treat me like one of your hired hands."'" This was the decision to go back home and cast himself on his father's mercy. Similarly, Zacchaeus's repentance was sacrificial. He took his ill-gotten wealth and gave it back, making sure that he repaid those he had defrauded in the process. While repentance is an initial turning, it is followed by behavior that exhibits the decision to seek a closer relationship with God.

In modern evangelism, one of the most crucial tasks of discernment is to discover the ways in which a non-Christian might be responding already to God's grace. If there are ways in which God is already inviting the person to turn away from a godless pattern of life and to seek a godly pattern, then the Christian evangelist should begin where the person already is and not impose another pattern or preconceived idea of what the person's starting point ought to be. Many persons have a longing for something in life that they cannot adequately name. When Christians say that everyone has a need for God that cannot be filled by anything else, it helps to name what the person is searching for.

In most cases it is important to distinguish between the person's felt need for God and what Scripture describes as the person's real need for God. God is not the product of human projections. God is God and comes to us from outside ourselves, revealing who we really are and what it truly means to be human. Reinhard Hütter's phrase, "suffering divine things," refers to his claim that human beings are called to be the subjects of God's creative activity, and that it is only by accepting God's working on us that we truly become free.[26]

If we understand the church, including individual evangelists, to be cooperating with the Holy Spirit in the work of bringing persons to repentance, then finding ways in which to connect with what God is already doing in the lives of persons is one of the first tasks of evangelism. Helping persons to discern how God's will intersects with their lives so that they can respond positively to God is a second step.

The process of repentance often involves trying out one or more of the seven aspects of Christian discipleship. Rarely do people turn their lives around completely at one instant. Rather, they may sense a need for God in their lives and start attending worship services. They may investigate Christian doctrine by joining a Bible study group or a class like Alpha.[27] They may get involved in building homes for poor persons or working to end capital punishment in their state. They may ask questions about different congregations, seeking friendship and community with people who will welcome them and give them the encouragement they need to continue their search for God. Yet, each of the seven aspects is more closely linked in a conceptual way to one of the other two steps of discipleship. Those steps will now be considered.

Justification

Justification is the point of entry into the Christian life where one's relationship to God changes. In the language of the New Testament, one becomes a child of God and is adopted as one of God's heirs. One becomes a new creature. Instead of being no people these persons become part of God's people. One leaves darkness and enters the light.[28] Wesley says, "Justification is another word for pardon. It is the forgiveness of all our sins, and (what is necessarily implied therein) our acceptance with God."[29] He refers to it as a relative change, one that alters a person's relationship with God. Once estranged, we are now accepted. In one metaphor Wesley compares religion to a house. Repentance is the porch, justification is the door, and sanctification is the whole house.[30]

BAPTISM

The theology underlying the two sacraments recognized by Protestant denominations poses some of the greatest points of controversy for a theology of evangelism. A variety of views are held on issues such as whether baptism is a means of grace or a symbol of it, whether infants may be baptized or not, and whether it should be done by immersion or by other means. Differing ecclesiologies have been associated with different understandings of baptism. At the same time, there is a strong consensus among Christians about baptism and its importance as a "sign of new life through Jesus Christ."[31] Given the long history of theological controversy and doctrinal divergence, what can be said about baptism's relation to evangelism?

Abraham's observation that baptism is a means of grace that should not be neglected in the process of initiation is helpful. He says that baptism is a source of spiritual renewal, and the rites of baptism and renewing of one's baptism, however understood, are significant ways in which new Christians are touched by God's grace. Christians may disagree about the precise understanding of baptism while still maintaining its centrality in the Christian life. It is normal for persons entering the Christian life to be baptized.

At the same time, while baptism is important and normative, it is not by itself sufficient. It is entirely possible for baptized persons to lose their faith, leave the church, and cease to be Christian disciples. Part of the significance of baptism is incorporation into the Body of Christ. There is no such thing as solitary Christianity. Real Christians are always connected with the church. For some this is expressed by being in communion with the church through participation in its sacraments. For others, this means weekly worship as part of a congregation. However the life of the community is defined, active participation in its life is required of all Christians.

Part of the problem facing genuine evangelism in the United States and other countries with a long history of Christian witness is that the meaning of entry into the Christian life has been debased. Too many people believe they can be good Christians and never attend worship or participate in the life of a congregation. Part of genuine evangelism is explaining that while some persons may indeed be saved without attending worship regularly, they are not Christian disciples. Discipleship means incorporation into a visible congregation and full participation in its corporate life.

I will argue in chapter 6 that persons who are already Christians should not be evangelized. Inviting persons to change from one congregation to another or from one denomination to another is not doing evangelism because they are not being initiated into Christian discipleship. However, if persons have become inactive without any sufficient reason, they have ceased to be Christian disciples and should be evangelized. In such a case, they are being re-initiated into Christian discipleship. They should never be rebaptized, but they should be invited to fulfill their baptism by re-entering the way of life that they began and then left.

Take the case of a baptized person who was confirmed and then as a teenager stopped attending worship. He is now forty-five years old and has not participated in any Christian activity for thirty years. There are no illnesses or physical limitations that prevent him from attending. He prefers to play golf and fish on Sundays. Whether his name is still on the membership role of his childhood congregation is irrelevant. What matters is that this person is no longer a Christian disciple because he does not follow the basic pattern of participating actively in a Christian congregation. Christians should regard him as a non-Christian who needs to receive a genuine invitation to recommit his life to Christ and participate in a church. He should not be rebaptized, but a ritual of remembering and reaffirming his baptism would be very appropriate if he recommits his life to Christ.

COGNITIVE COMMITMENTS

Another part of justification is the intellectual acceptance of the gospel. While faith is often defined as trusting or committing one's life to God, it also requires assent to the truth of the gospel, as much as one's cognitive abilities allow.[32] To become a Christian is to accept the church's claims about certain aspects of reality. Abraham says:

> It is platitudinous, moreover, to point out that announcing the dawning of the reign of God involves one in making a whole host of truth claims, both explicitly and implicitly. It presupposes, for example, that God exists, that the affairs of this world are seriously out of joint, that God has acted decisively in Jesus Christ to liberate the creation from bondage, that God acts here and now by the Holy Spirit to save, and so forth. To press this point would be to belabor the obvious. What is less obvious is that entering the reign of God commits one to a very particular intellectual heritage. As the kingdom has come in history it has evoked a specific theological tradition that cannot be set aside as secondary to the process of initiation.[33]

Abraham argues that there is genuine content to these truth claims expressed in the tradition of the church. His point is that when one enters the reign of God one comes to hold certain things as true.

Too many churches weaken Christian initiation by giving insufficient attention to doctrine. Some pretend not to have any doctrine at all, claiming to believe only the Bible. Others presuppose that a certain Christian consensus that was once widely agreed upon in the United States is still prevalent and that everyone knows the basic truths of Christianity. Instead, we have to acknowledge that the culture no longer carries the Christian message for us, and we must teach the basics of the faith to new believers as part of their initiation into discipleship.

The claim that new believers need to believe the basics of Christian doctrine is not the same as saying they need to be taught all of it. Further, it is possible to disagree with some of the teachings of the church while affirming the essential doctrines of the faith. The question then arises as to which doctrines are so basic that they need to be affirmed by new Christians?

Abraham proposes that a creed is a necessary supplement to the teaching of Scripture. Liturgically, many denominations ask persons to affirm the Nicene Creed at their baptism. Others use the Apostles' Creed. Abraham suggests that the Nicene Creed is superior to the Apostles' Creed because it was officially accepted by the early church and is most likely today to receive ecumenical endorsement.[34] In addition, one might add that in the present competition between Christianity and religions like the Church of Jesus Christ of Latter-day Saints, the Nicene Creed's more explicit teaching of the doctrine of the Trinity is important.

Inevitably, the question arises about the distinction between essential or basic doctrines that need to be affirmed as part of Christian initiation and those that are either less basic or less binding. Two answers can be given to this question. First, each denomination may determine for its own community which doctrines fall in each of these categories. Something like the Nicene Creed is a way to summarize the intellectual commitments thought to be so basic to the faith that a new convert should be able to affirm them at the time of his or her baptism. But some denominations may expect either more or less at this stage of the Christian life.

Second, there is a range of possible interpretations for many of these beliefs. Even within the most doctrinally strict denominations there is a continuing dialogue concerning how certain affirmations are best interpreted. Expecting uniformity of interpretation of doctrine is unrealistic, even if one expects uniform affirmation of the creedal formulation of doctrine. Hence, a variety of theologies within the church is important to its intellectual life. Only through such discussions of differing views can doctrinal development occur to meet new situations.[35] At the same time, clarity about basic doctrines is important to the church's unity and the vitality of its witness.

Sanctification

Justification is the moment of entry into the Christian life. At that moment, the process of sanctification begins. The New Testament characterizes sanctification in a variety of ways. Preeminently, it is becoming the kind of person who fulfills the Great Commandments—loving God with all of one's heart, mind, soul, and strength and one's neighbor as oneself (Mark12:30-31). But it is also having the mind which was in Christ Jesus (Phil. 2:5). It is being perfect as one's heavenly Father is perfect (Matt. 5:48). It is offering one's body as a living sacrifice and being transformed by the renewing of one's mind (Rom. 12:2). It is living by the Spirit and with its fruit

(Gal. 5:16, 22-23). It is obeying everything that Christ has commanded (Matt. 28:20).

The New Testament is clear that this level of Christian living is not achieved all at once upon one's entry into the Christian life. For example, some of the New Testament authors use the metaphor of running a race (Phil. 3:12-14, Heb. 12:1-2, 2 Tim. 4:7). Ephesians encourages each Christian to put on the whole armor of God (Eph. 6:10-17). Other texts speak of building each other up (1 Thess. 5:11).

With so many different metaphors from which to choose, it is sometimes difficult to get a comprehensive view of what is involved in Christian discipleship. Based on the Great Commandments, one can distinguish three objects of a life shaped by love. One loves God, oneself, and others. These three tasks can be distinguished as worship, formation, and witness. The difficulty is that all three of them are conceptually interrelated. Worshiping God is directly connected to spiritual formation and growth in one's love of self. Service to others is a form of self-giving which is the sort of spiritual worship Paul is referring to in Romans 12. Mission is spiritually formative, because sometimes the missionaries are the greatest recipients of the blessings involved in mission. After all, Jesus said that in losing our lives we find them (Matt. 10:39). Nevertheless, it is helpful to organize these three tasks of Christian initiation according to the primary objects of love.

WORSHIP

It has already been argued that in loving God, one of our first duties is to offer worship to God. As indicated in Acts, the Christian community from the earliest days under the apostles "devoted themselves to the apostles' teaching and fellowship, to the breaking of bread and the prayers" (Acts 2:42). In Matthew, when Jesus was tempted in the wilderness, he said, "Worship the Lord your God and serve only him" (Matt. 4:10). While all of the spiritual disciplines are forms of worship, corporate worship is the most basic of all. It is there that the Body of Christ is made visible and that the sacraments are celebrated.

Corporate worship is the most important way in which we fulfill the commandment to love God with our whole beings. By praising God, humbling ourselves in God's presence, confessing our sins, hearing God's word, and preparing ourselves to serve God in the world, we acknowledge that God is God and we are God's creatures. Leander Keck suggests that worship acknowledges what is true about God. He says, "In other words, God is to be praised because God is God, because of what God is and does, quite apart from what God is and does for me." He continues, "Since the Creator is praiseworthy, the creature has a moral obligation to acknowledge this with praise."[36] Marva Dawn has argued that too much worship today focuses on human need, whereas God is the object and subject of genuine worship. She quotes William Temple who defined worship as "the submission of all our nature to God. It is the quickening of the conscience by His holiness; the nourishment of the mind with His truth; the purifying of imagination by His beauty; the opening of the heart to His love; the surrender of will to His purpose—and all of this gathered up in adoration, the most selfless emotion of which our nature is capable."[37]

Dawn launches a strong argument against turning worship into "entertainment evangelism." She says:

> These attempts to reach out to persons who do not know God are certainly laudable—one would hope that we all look for ways to share our faith—but it is a misnomer to call services "worship" if their purpose is to attract people rather than to adore God. Plans for specific efforts to draw nonbelievers to the Church must be accompanied by definite preparations to move those attracted by such evangelistic rallies into services that actually worship God. The key is providing education for new believers to come to know God and what it means to worship.[38]

Dawn's own biases about what constitutes good music and thus facilitates authentic worship are often visible and detract from her argument, and yet her central thesis is right. Whatever enculturated form worship takes, it must retain its focus on loving God with one's whole self. Part of initiation into Christian discipleship is enabling new believers to genuinely worship God, not to be entertained.

Spiritual Disciplines: Eucharist, Prayer, and Fasting

Worship is thus the first and most important spiritual discipline. Others will be considered in the next section because they relate more to spiritual formation than to loving God. However, all of

these categories overlap because regular worship is in fact spiritually formative. In loving God we are also loving ourselves. In offering hospitality directed to others we are being spiritually formed to
be more giving and more Christlike. In the discipline of study, we
are prepared to love God more fully, to worship more authentically,
and to be more missional in our behavior toward others.

However, three of the spiritual disciplines that focus on our love
for God need to be considered briefly here. Eucharist is the sacrament whereby God's grace is communicated through the meal that
memorializes the Last Supper. Again, many churches have very
different theologies concerning what goes on in the Eucharist.
These disagreements extend to what role it plays in worship and
how often the sacrament should be celebrated. John Wesley understood Jesus' words "Do this in remembrance of me" to be a command that was to be obeyed as often as possible.[39] It is a means of
grace whereby God provides an ordinary channel of prevenient,
justifying, and sanctifying grace.[40] When the congregation prays
the Great Thanksgiving, it remembers God's mighty acts of salvation and offers praise to the Triune God. While celebration of the
Eucharist is a part of corporate worship, it is worth emphasizing
here precisely because too many congregations fail to celebrate it as
often as they should.

Likewise, prayer is a spiritual discipline that takes many forms,
including the corporate prayers of the community. However, private and family prayer are also important aspects of Christian discipleship that need to be emphasized. Jesus presumed his disciples
would pray. He said "When you pray . . . " (Matt. 6:7). Marjorie
Thompson notes, "The one condition that precedes *every* kind of
prayer is being present to God with conscious awareness. God is
always present with us, whether or not we can feel this reality. In a
very real sense, then, the foundation of all prayer is being present
to the presence of God."[41] She understands prayer as a conversation with God "that may cover a wide range of feelings and experiences, but we will generally express certain classic human
attitudes before God: praise, adoration, thanksgiving, confession,
and supplication."[42] In individual prayer, in family prayer, and in
the prayers offered by small groups of Christians, the church stays
in conversation with God and fulfills its duty of rendering to God
what belongs to God (see Matt. 22:21).

Fasting is a discipline that, once again, Jesus assumes his disciples will follow. He says, "And whenever you fast . . ." and then proceeds to describe how this discipline should be carried out (Matt. 6:16).[43] Thompson suggests that we need to recover the discipline of the fast because of the nature of modern culture. She writes:

> In a more tangible, visceral way than any other spiritual discipline, fasting reveals our excessive attachments and the assumptions that lie behind them. Food is necessary to life, but we have made it more necessary than God. How often have we neglected to remember God's presence when we would never consider neglecting to eat! Fasting brings us face to face with how we put the material world ahead of its spiritual Source.[44]

As with many other Christian practices, fasting can be misdirected. It can become a weight-loss gimmick or a means of proving spiritual superiority over others. Instead, it should be viewed as a means of grace by which the believer is directed to focus on God more than on material things.

FORMATION

Clearly, worship, Eucharist, prayer, and fasting are all formative. Yet, some Christian practices focus more on changing the person. These are the ones to be considered under the heading of formation.

Conversion

Abraham's discussion of conversion as a necessary aspect of initiation is very helpful. He summarizes it as follows:

> Through the action of the Holy Spirit, one is made acutely aware of one's sins, made conscious of the compassion of a holy God, and resolutely faced with the decision to choose either light or darkness, either life or death. To respond in a positive manner is not just one more decision in life, like deciding whether to have jam rather than marmalade on one's toast in the morning. It is to find oneself swept into a new relationship with God where one is acquitted of one's past and enters into a direct and unmediated kind of assurance. In such circumstances the language of new

birth is entirely natural and appropriate, for it captures a crucial dimension of what the innocent convert undergoes.[45]

In an important essay, José Miguez-Bonino argues that John Wesley's understanding of conversion needs to be updated. He observes that in the Methodist tradition from Wesley through the nineteenth century,

> the subjective consciousness is conceived as an individual and self-contained reality. The "religious transaction" takes place in "an inner sanctuary," "alone with God" as is frequently said. . . . In the last analysis it is the individual soul that is saved, sanctified, perfected. Fellowship is, at bottom, an *externum subsidium.* Such ideas are, to say the least, a fiction in the light of what we know today about human psychology—the subconscious, symbols, ideological mechanisms. Conscience (and self-consciousness) is not a "private area" but the focus of a complex process which includes historical relations—relations in time and space. Our self-consciousness is moulded by the social representations and the dominant symbols of a society (or of groups within it). Our "hearing" of a "message" is mediated by the "code" prevalent in our milieu. Any concrete "conversion" is a response to a *mediated* challenge, in which there is a certain self-understanding and a certain praxis already presupposed. Unless the challenge refers explicitly to such understandings and forms of behaviour it will automatically reinforce the presuppositions.[46]

Miguez then argues that conscientization, the process of self-awareness, is a crucial part of evangelism.

> Evangelism must, therefore, relate to the way in which human groups place themselves in the world, their visions of the world, their forms of social representation, their class and group consciousness, their forms of action. This means that conversion can take place either as a response to a verbally articulated message or to a specific communal praxis of the believers. In the last analysis, both things must happen.[47]

In some senses, the Christian community has always known that conversion includes altered behavior. To become a new creature means seeing the world in a different way and interacting with it in light of the will and the coming reign of God. Miguez is using the tools of modern social sciences to argue that the role of the community in shaping conversion experiences is more extensive than had been understood in recent Christian thinking.

Miguez's point adds to the understanding that conversion is one part of a holistic approach to evangelism. One's awareness of social location, justice issues, and the ways in which the people of God are bearing witness to the reign of God in all of its aspects are important. At the same time, individual conversion is also not to be neglected. There is a change when one enters the Christian life. To describe this as the new birth where one sees the world in ways previously unseen is a helpful, scriptural metaphor. Conversion involves a change in the intellect, in the emotions, and in one's allegiance to a community. While social influences are important, there is an inescapable individual dimension to it. Individuals live in communities and are shaped by them. But individuals also shape their communities. In postmodern culture, where the relationships between individuals and their communities are often matters of choice, the way in which individuals choose which communities to belong to becomes an important consideration.

Far too often churches foster a dichotomy between education and conversion. Congregations that favor the former stress the intellectual aspects of becoming a Christian and focus on the gradual nature of the process. Congregations that favor the latter often focus on emotional aspects and an instantaneous experience. An important study of conversions in eighteenth-century Methodism by Tom Albin points to a little-known fact. Methodists during this period of time were strong promoters of conversion and developed a system of oversight called the class meeting. In this system persons with "a desire to flee from the wrath to come" worked on the spiritual issues in their lives.[48] Albin consulted a number of primary sources and came to the conclusion that the average time between an individual's awakening to a need for salvation and the experience of conversion was twenty-eight months.[49] The stereotype of a person walking in to hear someone preach and immediately being transformed just does not hold up. Rather, education, spiritual formation, and conversion all work together to change the person's life. Sondra Higgins Matthaei has sought to heal this gap by writing about the ways in which education and conversion are congruent. Toward that end, she understands conversion "as a transformative experience through which lives are radically changed as persons come to know God's forgiveness and salvation through Jesus Christ and experience their adoption as children of God. Conversion encompasses both an experience of transformation *and* a lifelong endeavor of responding to God's redeeming grace through faithful discipleship." [50] She is describing what she elsewhere calls "an ecology of faith formation" that aims to make disciples.[51]

It is important to emphasize that conversion is not an end in itself. Too often, persons have characterized evangelism as being focused on soul-winning. It is not the aim of Christian evangelism to convert people. Rather, the aim of evangelism is to make disciples of Jesus Christ, and conversion is one part of that process. David Bosch understands Luke's Gospel as making this point. He writes:

> Conversion does not pertain merely to an individual's act of conviction and commitment; it moves the individual believer into the community of believers and involves a real—even a radical—change in the life of the believer, which carries with it moral responsibilities that distinguish Christians from "outsiders" while at the same time stressing their obligation to those "outsiders."[52]

Conversion is the change in a person's heart that is correlated with entry into a new way of life. All other aspects of Christian discipleship constitute this way of life. In being converted, the believer is transformed and participates in this new way of life with the whole self. As the new believer makes progress toward Christian maturity, there are multiple conversions as the individual gives more and more of the self to Christ.

Spiritual Disciplines: Study and Fellowship

Spiritual formation includes the disciplines of study and fellowship. The most important aspect of study is regular engagement with Scripture. The authority of Scripture requires that Christians know the text and that they accept its function as mediating God's revelation. The Bible needs to be read and understood. It is the responsibility of each Christian to know what it says and to know what it does not say.

However, the community must also address the way in which the Bible is read. In their book, *Liberation Preaching,* Catherine and Justo González call for an end to "Lone-Ranger Bible Study." They observe:

> But the problem is that most of the Bible was written to be read, not in private, but in public, often within the context of corporate worship. Just as it is not the same to read a sermon as it is to hear it preached, it is not the same to read the Bible in private as it is to read it and hear it being read in the midst of the people of God. The Lone-Ranger student of the Bible loses a great deal that cannot be regained by any amount of study or private devotion.[53]

A similar point is made by Stephen Fowl and Gregory Jones. They argue persuasively that there is a wide and irreducible variety of meanings of the biblical text saying, "Academic biblical scholars in particular have engaged in a persistent quest for a method which an isolated autonomous individual can use to uncover 'the meaning' of a text regardless of whether any specific use will be made of the text."[54] They continue, "Rather than pursue this illusory quest for the meaning of a text, we recommend that we think in terms of 'interpretive interests.' One can pursue any number of interpretive interests; we can rationally evaluate the results of such pursuits; and we need never call these results 'the meaning of the text.'"[55] Fowl and Jones understand Christian interpretation as an activity of the church.

> Christian communities interpret Scripture, then, so that believers might live faithfully before God in the light of Jesus Christ. The aim of faithful living before the Triune God becomes the standard to which all interpretive interests must measure up. One cannot begin to judge whether this standard is being achieved unless and until the interpretation of Scripture becomes socially embodied in communities of people committed to ordering their worship, their doctrines, and their lives in a manner consistent with faithful interpretation.[56]

Fowl and Jones are arguing that using Scripture for Christian ethics involves the whole life of the community. In its life together the Bible is read, discussed, and applied by the community. Scripture shapes the community, while at the same time the life of the community shapes its understanding of the sacred text. Christian fellowship includes participation in the full range of activities of the Body of Christ. In this sense, fellowship is a spiritual discipline. It should not be understood as a shallow pattern of potluck dinners and parties. Rather, participation in the Christian community should shape a person's life and orient the community's members toward the whole range of different aspects of Christian discipleship. For example, when the Christian community celebrates a fiftieth wedding anniversary for two of its members, the speeches, congratulatory letters, food, and prayer of thanksgiving are powerful affirmations of the possibility and importance of marriage. When the community takes on the building of a Habitat for Humanity house, the activity shapes the lives of all who participate. The persons hammering, the persons who pay for the materials, the persons fixing lunch for the workers, those praying for the family that will live there, the children who watch the workers, and the persons loading building materials into pickup trucks all learn that being a Christian involves sacrificial care for the poor. Participation in Christian community in all of its aspects is a formative way of life.

WITNESS

Third, sanctification has to do with the way Christians love others. In connecting the two Great Commandments the way he did, Jesus implied that loving others is intrinsically related to loving God. David Bosch's reading of the New Testament as a missionary document leads to his view that the Christian faith is "intrinsically missionary." He claims that "the entire Christian existence is to be characterized as missionary existence."[57] Part of this mission is the task of bearing witness, that is, of sharing the love of God with others. This means that every Christian must understand herself or himself as a missionary. Christians were told by Christ to bear witness in Jerusalem and to the ends of the earth (Acts 1:8). It was a mistake when Christians regarded their home territory as anything other than a mission field. All Christians are called to bear witness in all places because Christ died for all persons.

Morality

The category of morality could be considered as encompassing all of the Christian life. In an important sense the whole point of loving God through worship and loving oneself through formation is aimed at fulfilling God's commands to become the fully human persons God has created us to be.

Here, though, I want to consider morality in a more narrow aspect, that of loving others. Salvation comes by faith, but when faith has time and opportunity one of the ways it manifests itself is by active love of neighbor. Such good works are a response to the reign of God that takes the form of avoiding sin and embracing all that is good.

Becoming a disciple thus means that certain practices are left behind because they are immoral, while others are embraced. For example, consider a business man who is systematically cheating his customers by installing inferior parts in the equipment he sells while at the same time underpaying his employees. By becoming a Christian, he must commit to honesty, integrity, and concern for others in all of his relationships, including his business.

The sphere of morality applies as well to issues of social justice. To be a disciple of Jesus is to commit one's life to following the one who taught the parable of the sheep and the goats in Matthew 25:31-46. Christian discipleship must include action and advocacy on behalf of "the least of these." Such activities may include supporting a food pantry with time and money as well as lobbying one's government for a more equitable system of distributing health-care services.

When a self-avowed, practicing sinner becomes a disciple, the church must make it clear that Christian discipleship entails an end to all immoral practices. The dishonest businessperson must embrace fair practices, the rich must give to the poor, racists must embrace those with different skin color, and the powerful must take action on behalf of the oppressed.

This approach to the moral life is summarized in the first two of Wesley's three general rules. In eighteenth-century Methodist practice, persons who had a desire to be saved, were expected to follow the "General Rules." Membership in the Society was contingent on showing the works that were appropriate for each stage of salvation. Whoever desired to "flee from the wrath to come" was welcome. Wesley continues:

> But wherever this [desire] is really fixed in the soul it will be shown by its fruits. It is therefore expected of all who continue

therein that they should continue to evidence their desire of salvation,

First, By doing no harm, by avoiding evil of every kind—especially that which is most generally practised. . . .

Secondly, By doing good, by being in every kind merciful after their power, as they have opportunity doing good of every possible sort and as far as possible to all men.[58]

Wesley knew that salvation came by faith, but that through faith God also circumcised the heart so that works of piety and works of mercy would follow. The goal of the Christian life is to be so filled with love that all of one's intentional actions are motivated by love of God and love of neighbor.

Many churches have statements of their social principles where they teach their understanding of the Christian position on social issues. Part of the difficulty of contemporary Christian life is the lack of consensus among Christians about some moral issues. Given the cultural turmoil of the last third of the twentieth century, such debate and disagreement is inevitable. In this context, each community must do its best to discern how to teach and embody the highest levels of commitment to loving one's neighbor in accordance with Christ's commandments.

In the midst of such controversy, it has often been tempting to avoid making moral judgments altogether and so to lower the standards of Christian discipleship that the moral aspect is almost never mentioned. Instead, I have argued that initiation into Christian discipleship makes clear demands on how persons live their lives. Becoming a disciple means that certain practices are no long permissible and other practices are now required. The precise form that takes will vary given the differing perspectives within the Body of Christ. But that there should be some moral aspect of discipleship is essential.

Spiritual Gifts

Abraham's analysis of the importance of life in the Holy Spirit is a helpful reminder to mainline Christians that they need to pay more attention to this topic. At two points the New Testament speaks explicitly of different gifts given by the Holy Spirit.

Ephesians 4:11-13 says, "The gifts he gave were that some would be apostles, some prophets, some evangelists, some pastors and teachers, to equip the saints for the work of ministry, for building up the body of Christ, until all of us come to the unity of the faith and of the knowledge of the Son of God, to maturity, to the measure of the full stature of Christ." Similarly, in 1 Corinthians 12, Paul employs the metaphors of spiritual gifts as well as diversity in a body to argue that different gifts should work together for the good of the whole.

A number of factors suggest that, in Lyle Dabney's words, pneumatology is "the unfinished business of the Protestant theological tradition." [59] It is a major agenda for theological reflection about Christian discipleship. The explosion of Pentecostal movements in Latin America and Africa point to a changing reality for the future of Christianity.

We should take seriously the idea that every Christian receives one or more gifts from the Holy Spirit. However, the purposes of the gifts are missional. They are intended to be used to build up the Body of Christ and to strengthen its missionary work in the world. If gifts are used without love, they are nothing (1 Cor. 13:1-3). Interpretation of someone speaking in tongues is more important than the original speaking (1 Cor. 14:5). Sometimes, the phenomena of spiritual gifts are abused as a sign of one's Christian profession or one's progress toward Christian maturity. Viewed from a missional perspective, the important thing about spiritual gifts is how they are being used to serve the reign of God in the world.

Spiritual Disciplines: Hospitality

The practice of hospitality is rooted in specific commandments in Scripture. It is one of the ways in which Christians are called to love persons. This is made clear in Hebrews 13:1-2, which reads, "Let mutual love continue. Do not neglect to show hospitality to strangers, for by doing that some have entertained angels without knowing it." In Romans 12:9-13, the command to show hospitality to strangers comes in a list of commandments, which begins with "let love be genuine."

Marjorie Thompson counts hospitality as one of the spiritual disciplines Christians are called to practice. She says, "Hospitality means receiving the other, from the heart, into my own dwelling place. It entails providing for the need, comfort, and delight of the other with all the openness, respect, freedom, tenderness, and joy that love itself embodies."[60] While Thompson does not make a connection between this practice and evangelism, such a move is easily made when one understands that the non-Christian guest needs a relationship with Christ. Providing a genuine invitation to know Christ and become part of Christ's body, the church, is a significant act of hospitality. However, her other qualifications introduce important ways of understanding evangelistic hospitality as an act of love. Such an invitation needs to involve respect, freedom, and tenderness or else it is not genuine hospitality.

A missionary congregation must practice the discipline of reaching out to the world to help transform it in the name of Christ. At the same time, it must be a place of hospitality, welcoming new persons who join the community. When newcomers are initiated into the community's life, it must send them out again into the world as missionaries to represent Christ in their workplace, in their families, in their neighborhoods, and at school. Thus, while the spiritual discipline of hospitality may appear to be inwardly focused, when seen as welcoming the stranger into the life of the community it is actually another act of missionary outreach.

Faith-Sharing

The aspect of discipleship not addressed adequately in Abraham's analysis is the role of each disciple in verbally sharing his or her faith with others. The most effective evangelists are not clergy. They are laypersons who give their testimony in appropriate ways when engaged in everyday conversation with their friends, relatives, associates at work, and neighbors. When religious topics come up in conversation or when the religious aspect of a topic could easily be introduced, laypersons should know that sharing their faith in Christ is an act of love. This models for others the possibility that they might come to believe in Christ, too.

One can distinguish three levels of faith-sharing. At its most basic level, faith-sharing is simply the invitation to attend worship or Sunday school. The expectation is that these are means of grace, and inviting non-Christians to attend enhances the possibility of their encountering the reign of God. A second level of faith-sharing is to give one's testimony, that is, to describe what God has done in one's life. This could be in private conversation or in front of a group. The third and most specialized way of faith-sharing is to be in deep, sustained conversation with someone about their making a commitment to Christ. This kind of discipling conversation takes patience, good listening abilities, and a clear understanding of the faith so that one can act as a midwife to the birth of faith in another. But in all three of these, the laity are often more effective and more credible than the clergy.

Many persons argue that people attend church for the first time because they were invited to do so. Persons who are not part of a Christian community often feel like they are not wanted or not included, and so they look for happiness in other places that are more welcoming. Simply inviting one's non-Christian friends to attend a worship service, Bible study, or workday to build a home for a poor family is a way of helping them experience God's grace as it is being made visible in the life of the church.

Every Christian has a verbal witness to share with others. Finding ways of doing that "with gentleness and reverence" is a challenge, but it is a necessary task (1 Pet. 3:16). At the same time there are more specialized gifts. The ability to disciple others and to lead them to make a Christian commitment is the gift of being an evangelist in the more narrow sense of the word. Many people have deep questions about the faith, and they need to be talked through the intellectual, moral or emotional obstacles that prevent them from making a commitment to Christ. They often need a knowledgeable or sympathetic friend who can guide them through that experience. These persons are often gifted to serve as leaders of small groups in which seekers can process the issues before making a commitment. Sharing one's faith in a small group and giving a testimony before a large crowd are both gifts that are needed for the overall health of the Christian community.[61]

CHAPTER FOUR

Evangelism as Initiation into Christian Discipleship

Everything that has been argued so far in this book has aimed at answering the question, "What is evangelism?" The argument began by showing that evangelism was deeply tied to the gospel, and that the understanding of the gospel is rooted in how the wholeness of Scripture is construed. The centrality of God's saving love for creation and especially for humankind leads to the coming of Christ and the proclamation of the reign of God. The appropriate response to the reign of God is Christian discipleship, which is centered around loving God and loving neighbor and loving self. The logic of discipleship was then analyzed as falling into three steps—repentance, justification, and sanctification. In turn, sanctification was seen as having three tasks—worship, formation, and mission. Understood in this way, Christian discipleship has seven aspects: baptism, cognitive commitments, spiritual disciplines, conversion, morality, spiritual gifts, and faith-sharing.

Definitional Problems

It is a commonplace in scholarly studies of evangelism to observe that there is little agreement on how to define "evangelism" and thus great confusion in discussing its practice. David Barrett says that Francis Bacon was the first to use the word in 1626 and that Samuel Johnson's 1755 dictionary gave it the definition "promulgation of the blessed gospel."[1] However, the word remained largely unused until the nineteenth century, and according to Barrett it did not come into widespread use in English-speaking Christianity until 1920.[2] Its cognate "evangelist" was used most often to refer to the authors of the four Gospels and occasionally to the office of evangelist mentioned in Ephesians 4:11 or in connection with Philip and Timothy in discussions of Acts 21:8 and 2 Timothy 4:5. "Evangelization" was coined in 1651 by Thomas Hobbes. After 1850 the term gained widespread usage, most notably by the Student Volunteer Movement for Foreign Missions. After an 1886 conference in Northfield, Massachusetts, the organization was formed, and their watchword was "the evangelization of the world in this generation."[3] Barrett's comprehensive study details how the terms "evangelism" and "evangelization" have been used by both Protestants and Roman Catholics during the last two hundred years with a variety of meanings.

Mission and Evangelism

One of the most fundamental problems surrounding the definition of evangelism is clarifying its relationship with mission. This has been a subject of great disagreement. In *Transforming Mission,* Bosch says:

> Some suggest that "mission" has to do with ministry to people (particularly those in the Third World) who are *not yet* Christians and "evangelism" with ministry to those (particularly in the West) who are *no longer* Christians. The existence of such "no longer" Christians reflects a new situation. Prior to the Enlightenment and the Age of Discovery all people outside the West were "pagans," whereas everybody in the West was considered Christian. Now there are "non-believers" in the West also.[4]

Bosch's earlier essay "Mission and Evangelism" outlines twelve different positions of how mission and evangelism are seen today.[5] One position equates mission with evangelism, and both are viewed as winning souls for eternity. A middle position holds that evangelism and social action are both important, but they are genuinely distinct and should not be prioritized. Another extreme position on this spectrum is that mission and evangelism are the same, but they are viewed as humanization or social action.

Bosch seeks to combine several of these positions into a new one. In eighteen points, he clarifies his position, which can be summarized by five statements. First, mission is wider than evangelism, and therefore not to be equated with it. Second, evangelism is an essential dimension of mission. Third, evangelism is witnessing to what God has done, is doing, and will do that aims at a response. Fourth, evangelism is always contextual and relates to the preaching and practice of justice. Fifth, evangelism is more than verbal proclamation.[6]

The position that has been outlined so far in this book fully corresponds with Bosch's position. The church's mission is wider than evangelism and includes all that God expects the church to do. At the same time, evangelism is an essential part of mission; when there is no evangelistic component the missionary activity is inadequate. As will be shown below, evangelism takes many different forms, including both words and deeds.

A Plethora of Definitions

John R. Mott was a layperson who held numerous significant leadership positions in the Student Volunteer Movement, the YMCA, and the World Council of Churches. In preparation for the 1938 World Christian Conference held at Tambaram, Madras, India, he asked three questions of "recognized authorities and participants in the vital work of evangelism." He asked:

> 1. How would you define evangelism? In other words, in the light of your own thought, observation, and experience, what does this subject signify to you? 2. In the fields with which you are most familiar, what aspects of the Christian Gospel are most relevant in these days? 3. Within the range of your experience, or of your intimate observation and knowledge, what has characterized

the work of evangelism which has been most fruitful in deeply satisfying and abiding results?[7]

He received 125 replies, which he characterized as "fairly representative of Older and Younger Churches, of various cultures and schools of thought, and of wide outlook and rich experience."[8] He then reprinted the most relevant portions of the replies. While Mott finds a "large degree of unanimity," he concludes:

> The final impression is one of the inability to express adequately the height and depth of all that is involved in this God-given undertaking. One is reminded of an expression of St. Paul, the great master of expression of the hidden depths of meaning of the wondrous mission of Christ to men. As much as to say, it is hopeless to try to convey in human language the full meaning of the Gospel and its transmission, he breaks out with the exclamation, "Thanks be to God for His *unspeakable* Gift."[9]

These replies raise many different issues that defy categorization. While they most often refer to proclamation, they also make reference to evangelism as the art of persuasion, witnessing, and using one's life as a silent form of proclamation.

The diversity of definitions can be accounted for in another way. I argued at the beginning of this book that evangelism was both theologically and etymologically tied to the gospel of Jesus Christ. In defining evangelism, one is defining a term that reflects one's whole understanding of God, salvation, ecclesiology, and eschatology. Given the diversity of different Christian churches and different contexts, it is not surprising that Mott could find 125 different definitions.

Evangelism as Process or Product?

Darius Salter has analyzed the 79 definitions (out of Mott's 125) included in Barrett's *Evangelize!* and he finds that they can be divided according to their emphasis on evangelism as a process or a product. As an example of the former, he cites E. Stanley Jones, who says, "Evangelism is the Good News of the Kingdom of God on earth, that Kingdom personalized and embodied in Christ." Another example is "Making known to men the message of salvation."[10] On the other side of this typology are those statements that emphasize the end result. Henry Sloane Coffin wrote, "Evangelism should be defined as the presentation of the Gospel of Christ in such wise as to win immediately loyalty to Him." William Temple's contribution was "the winning of men to acknowledge Christ as their Savior and King, so that they give themselves to His service in the fellowship of His Church." Salter says, "Such descriptions add the dimension of actual change that takes place in the life of the hearers. Change is predicated upon positive acceptance of the message by the recipient."[11]

Salter criticizes the process definitions, including the view of J. I. Packer that "our calculating, pragmatic and rationalistic age has caused us to lose sight of God's mystery and wisdom." Packer defines evangelism saying, "According to the New Testament, evangelism is just preaching the gospel, the evangel. It is a work of communication in which Christians make themselves mouthpieces for God's message of mercy to sinners."[12] Without rebutting Packer's argument or dealing with it in a serious way, he then calls it defective. He says such definitions, "leave no room for the evaluation of effectiveness. Packer has difficulty reconciling the use of human reason and giving proper credit to God's sovereign grace."[13] Rather than rebutting Packer, Salter illustrates the point. His concern for evaluation, for trustworthy methods, and for the evaluation of results reflects the modern fascination with cause and effect. Finney's classic *Lectures on Revival* perhaps made this point most clearly. Revival is not a miracle. Instead, it is the right exercise of the powers of nature. For Finney, while God's blessing gives growth to the seed, the growth is not miraculous, and it is the same with using the means for a revival. "The connection between the right use of means for a revival and a revival is as philosophically sure as between the right use of means to raise grain and a crop of wheat."[14]

The problem with focusing on product is the negation of God's sovereign freedom and the liberty of human beings. On the one hand, no one can predict where the Holy Spirit will go.[15] In the argument I have advanced thus far, this is shown in the priority given to God's mission and God's saving activity, of which human evangelistic efforts are simply a part. On the other hand, when the seed of the gospel is scattered, the results vary. Jesus noted in his parable that "a sower went out to sow his seed; and as he sowed, some fell on the path and was trampled on, and the birds of the air ate it up. Some fell on the rock; and as it grew up, it withered for lack of moisture. Some fell among thorns, and the thorns grew with it and choked it. Some fell into good soil, and when it grew it, produced a hundredfold" (Luke 8:5-8). The point is that there is a radical uncertainty about how individuals, cultural conditions, and many other factors—including the workings of the enemy—will affect how the work of evangelism is received.

If an evangelist does everything right to the best of his or her abilities, is it certain that the person being evangelized will respond positively? Of course not. The recipient may prefer darkness to light and choose not to serve God (John 3:20). The recipient may not fully understand the message. The recipient may not be ready to make a commitment, but may need more time to discern whether this invitation is the correct way of life. Cultural and social factors may interfere. The idea that excellent performance of the ministry of evangelism guarantees positive responses places too much emphasis on the agency of the evangelist. Excellence on the part of the evangelist and faithfulness on the part of God do not mean that the others will cooperate.

Hence, it is important that evangelism be conceived as a process that aims at a product. The results are left undetermined. Ideally, the seed bears fruit. But sometimes seeds go years without sprouting, and other times things happen that prevent the seed from germinating. Yet, the sower has faithfully done his or her job. To carry the analogy further, this does not mean that the sower intentionally sows without any concern for results. The sower's intention is to get a harvest. So, the intentionality of the evangelist will be a crucial component in our definition of this ministry.

Evangelism and Church Growth

The most sophisticated advocates of the view that evangelism is aimed at results are Donald McGavran and Peter Wagner. Their *Understanding Church Growth* deserves careful study. McGavran and Wagner define mission "as an enterprise devoted to proclaiming the good news of Jesus Christ, and to persuading men and women to become his disciples and responsible members of his church."[16] They are deeply concerned about the fate of lost persons. "Anyone who would comprehend the growth of Christian churches must see it primarily as faithfulness to God. God desires it. Christians, like their Master, are sent to seek and save the lost."[17] Finding the lost occurs through the multiplication of churches. They suggest we need hard facts about the reachable groups in the world so that the unnecessary cultural barriers between them and the gospel might be lowered. Research on growing churches can show the causes of their growth.[18]

The chief advantage of this approach is McGavran and Wagner's focus on the contextual realities of each situation and the experience of what actually works in helping bring persons to Christ. They understand very well that evangelism is about helping persons enter into the Christian life.

One of the principal weaknesses of their approach, however, is that instead of seven aspects they see evangelism as simply conversion and incorporation into the church. The rest they leave to the process of discipling. However, when one leaves so many things to a later stage, they often suffer from neglect. It is far better to describe all seven aspects of Christian discipleship and insist on a full-bodied initiation into all seven.

Perhaps the best expression of this church-growth school of thought is George G. Hunter, III's *Church for the Unchurched*. There Hunter briefly describes modern America as secular and postmodern. But he sees this as a new age of opportunity that is being met well by "apostolic" congregations. These churches share four characteristics:

> (1) Their leaders believe that they and the church are "called" and "sent" by God to reach an unchurched pre-Christian population. (2) Their theology and message center upon the gospel of early apostolic Christianity, rather than upon the narrower dogmatism, or the more vague "inclusive" theism, or the conventional moralism found in many traditional churches. (3) Like the early apostles and their communities, these churches adapt to the language and the culture of their target population to communicate meaningfully the meaning of the ancient message. (4) They are remarkably similar to certain key features we find in early apostolic Christianity, in the Anabaptist, Pietist, and Methodist apostolic

movements within Reformation Christianity and in many growing Third World congregations today.[19]

Hunter found nine congregations whose growth is due to principles rather than the personality of the pastor. He excluded those
that emphasize the "prosperity gospel" or "super-patriotism."[20]
While he could have broadened his sample, limited time and travel
budget restricted his research. More important, he found he was
"meeting the same principles over and over, and telephone conversations with leaders of some of the other churches revealed that
further research would have been redundant."[21] Hunter makes
many references to "reaching unchurched persons" and says he
wants to ask, "What kind of church can reach and disciple the
growing number of secular people across the land?"[22] His empirical research methodology led him to identify these nine congregations and then inductively to determine the principles that they
hold in common.

The strength of Hunter's study lies precisely in his descriptive
approach to studying congregations that he believes are doing
evangelism well. By examining Frazer Memorial United Methodist
Church, New Hope Community Church, Willow Creek
Community Church, Community Church of Joy, Saddleback Valley
Community Church, The Church on Brady, New Song Church,
Ginghamsburg United Methodist Church, and Vineyard
Community Church he has a database that is plausible to many of
his readers. These congregations are widely recognized as being
successful. Their pastors lead conferences where they seek to share
their experiences and teach others how to grow. Several of them
have written books that have sold well. Several of them sponsor
meetings where clergy and laity can visit their congregations and
learn how to do evangelism.

Yet Hunter's greatest weakness is precisely his strength. By
focusing on large churches that are successful in numerical terms,
he opens himself to the criticism that his sample is skewed. Are
only large churches apostolic? Can a congregation in western
Kansas be apostolic? Why are there not more Asian, black, or
Hispanic congregations included in his sample?

Still, the ten principles he claims to have derived inductively
from the sample are plausible. They are as follows:

1. Apostolic Congregations take a redundant approach to rooting believers and seekers in Scripture.

2. Apostolic Congregations are disciplined and earnest in Prayer, and they expect and experience God's action in response.

3. Apostolic Congregations understand, like, and have compassion for lost, unchurched, pre-Christian people.

4. Apostolic Congregations obey the Great Commission— more as warrant or privilege than mere duty. Indeed, their main business is to make faith possible for unreached people; evangelization is not merely one of many more or less equally important ministries of the church.

5. Apostolic congregations have a motivationally sufficient vision for what people, as disciples, can become.

6. Apostolic congregations adapt to the language, music and style of the target population's culture.

7. Apostolic congregations labor to involve everyone, believers and seekers, in small groups.

8. Apostolic congregations prioritize the involvement of all Christians in lay ministries for which they are gifted.

9. The members of Apostolic Congregations receive regular pastoral care. They are in regular spiritual conversation with someone who is gifted for shepherding ministry.

10. Apostolic Congregations engage in many ministries to unchurched non-Christian people.[23]

Two questions arise. First, can the same principles be derived from theological considerations without focusing on specific congregations that allow for the charge of bias? Second, would careful theological reflection on the gospel point out ways in which these nine congregations are "not perfect churches"? Hunter affirms this is true of the congregations studied, but he does not discuss their inadequacies.[24]

Of Hunter's ten principles, he acknowledges that the first four are rather obvious. He calls them "hunches" though, and says that they are confirmed by the practices of these congregations. The importance of Scripture, prayer, loving lost people, and joyfully obeying the Great Commission are in fact theological principles that are derived from a particular reading of Scripture and theological traditions based upon Scripture. To claim these as hunches belies their theological grounding in the gospel. Because of this, the ways in which scripture is read in these nine congregations and the theological justifications for such readings are obscured.

The pragmatism of Hunter's work thus obscures the important theological debate and insight emerging out of these congregations. Why do they read Scripture the way they do, and why should their reading be normative for other congregations? Hunter's answer appears to be that it works, and therefore these congregations are worthy of imitation. He claims that they are "apostolic" because they follow closely the practices and doctrines of the New Testament church and other apostolic movements in Christian history. But this assumes a particular answer to the question about what the apostolic model is and why these four practices, with which few persons would disagree, are truly apostolic as they are being practiced today. One can imagine Orlando Costas and Mortimer Arias looking at these nine congregations and arguing that they are not apostolic because of their neglect of marginalized persons and their failure to deal explicitly with the political implications of God's reign. One can argue that other practices of the early church such as episcopacy, priesthood, and weekly Eucharist are more central to the definition of "apostolic" than Hunter allows. Hunter does not offer historical arguments about the nature of the apostolic church. He further does not specify how Scripture authorizes these principles. Instead, it appears that significant growth in numbers is the primary criterion of apostolicity.

The six principles with which Hunter deals at some length are a mixture of unexamined theological claims and contextually driven judgments. He writes, "A motivationally sufficient vision for what people, as disciples, can become" is grounded in the proclamation of God's love for persons and God's desire that they become fully human in obedience to God's will. "Motivationally sufficient" means that this biblical vision has been communicated in such a way to make it credible to contemporary men and women. The claim that the gospel must be enculturated is a deeply theological claim, while the argument that language, music, and style are the most important aspects of enculturation may be driven by the particular realities of Hunter's target audiences. The claim that small groups are an essential part of Christian practice is clearly driven by the contexts he is addressing, since small group ministry has not always been a part of apostolic Christian practice. The ministry of the laity and the importance of pastoral care are clearly theological claims, while his descriptions of how they are carried out is contextually driven. The last principle, the view that there need to be many ministries to unchurched, non-Christian people is again a theological judgment based on New Testament anthropology and the multifaceted character of initiation into Christian discipleship.

Hunter's judgments are helpful, but need to be put in proper theological perspective. Walter Brueggemann's comment about church growth is instructive. He says:

> Evangelism is related *to church growth*, related but in no way synonymous. In speaking of evangelism, one must speak of church growth, but only at the end of the dramatic process, and not any sooner. Evangelism is never aimed at institutional enhancement or aggrandizement. It is aimed simply and solely at summoning people to new, liberated obedience to the true governor of all created reality. . . . "Church growth" misserves evangelism, however, when the church is allied with consumerism, for then the church talks people out of the very obedience to which the news summons us.[25]

One of the chief ways Christianity has been corrupted is in confusing the welfare of the institutional church with the welfare of the reign of God. Thus, large churches with big attendance and large budgets and large staffs are presumed to be discipling persons well. However, the theological questions about what constitutes faithful discipleship in a particular context are often ignored in favor of large numbers.

All of this is not to render judgments about the nine congregations Hunter describes. They may in fact be doing very well at discipling persons in their contexts. The problem comes with the way the description is rendered by selecting these nine on the basis of growth without adequate consideration of the theological visions that drive each of them.

If the theological concerns were put first, then there would be a different approach to how the principles are presented and a more adequate ground for considering the strengths and shortcomings of these congregations. Church growth would be seen as an intended, though not guaranteed, outcome of faithful evangelism. Further, a theological critique of the evangelistic faithfulness of the congregations being studied would examine their shortcomings as well. In what ways are these congregations failing to serve the gospel? A concern for social justice is notably absent from Hunter's account. If each of the nine exemplary congregations is in fact addressing issues such as materialism, racism, sexism, sexual immorality, and drug/alcohol abuse in American culture, then these concerns are not present in his analysis. Adam Hamilton's account of the principles driving The United Methodist Church of the Resurrection would fit easily within Hunter's paradigm of an apostolic church. Yet, he speaks explicitly about the ways they have addressed many contemporary social issues.[26] Any account of Windsor Village United Methodist Church would have to look at the ways in which Kirbyjon Caldwell has addressed social justice issues in Houston, Texas. At the same time, any congregation is open to critique on the basis that it is not doing as much as it should in these areas. One suspects that the nine exemplary churches Hunter uses as models are also engaged in these ministries, and that Hunter's lack of an explicitly theological orientation has led him to overlook the evangelistic importance of this aspect of the church's ministry.

Evangelism as Proclamation?

Two recent books on evangelism make significant contributions to the field while employing an understanding of evangelism as proclamation. Kevin Ruffcorn's *Rural Evangelism: Catching the Vision* offers a contextualized analysis of the problems and opportunities facing rural congregations. He shows how small, rural churches can do effective evangelism. With regard to defining evangelism, he discusses it as proclamation, but does so in ways that confuse the reader. He begins his consideration of the term by giving a "Sunday-school" view that it is "proclamation of the good news."[27] He says that "proclamation" means simply "to announce." Yet, he goes on to say, "It goes without saying, yet still needs to be stressed, that evangelism includes both the spoken word and the lived life."[28] This prepares the way for his complete definition: "Evangelism is the proclamation of the good news, both inwardly and outwardly, by word and action, in an intentional and relational manner."[29]

The problem with this definition comes with seeing evangelism as proclamation by word and deed. If "to proclaim" has the same meaning as "to announce," the strongest connotations are with a verbal understanding of both words. How does one announce something by deeds? This is a metaphorical use of the word that leads to unnecessary confusion. If proclamation and announcement are both seen as verbal activities, then one can restate his view of evangelism to say that the announcement must be accompanied by deeds in order for the message to be credible.

Walter Klaiber gives more consideration to this issue and points out the source of the idea that evangelism is proclamation. He says that biblical terminology sets this approach, resting as it does on *euangelizesthai*. He says about evangelism:

> The term has its origins in a biblical verb of speech. It lives from its contents, from the message, which it proclaims. This message and its orientation have a fundamental and elementary character. This means that its task involves more than the verbal mediation of its commission; rather it seeks communication with all the dimensions of human life and human need. Nonetheless, evangelism as word event is the "heart" of mission in so far as it names what saves and liberates humankind and that from which the Christian community and its members live.[30]

Both Klaiber and Ruffcorn emphasize the verbal understanding of evangelism as proclamation while acknowledging nonverbal dimensions as well.

There are two crucial problems in defining evangelism as proclamation. First, those writers such as Ruffcorn and Klaiber who describe proclamation as including deeds as well as words have confused the discussion. "To proclaim" carries explicitly verbal connotations. When persons quote Francis of Assisi as saying, "Preach the gospel always. Use words if necessary," the power of the aphorism rests precisely on the paradox of preaching silently. To proclaim is to use the spoken word. Thus, to define evangelism as proclamation, despite disclaimers seeking to broaden the meaning of the term, leads to confusion.

The second problem arises from the first. There are a wide variety of actions that might help a person experience the reign of God and lead them to enter into Christian discipleship. Proclamation, even in the broadest understanding of the term, cannot cover all of these activities. Healing, social action, painting the church building, welcoming a first-time visitor, denouncing injustice, and many other forms of Christian witness may help initiate persons into Christian discipleship. To call all of them "proclamation" makes the term vacuous. Further, because there has often been a focus on the spoken word as the main evangelistic activity, seeking to define all of these as proclamation leads to devaluing the importance of nonspoken methods of evangelism. It is far better to give all of the methods a significant place in evangelism by using a more general, inclusive term. While evangelism has an essentially verbal element, it must be much more than verbal because it must mediate an encounter with the reign of God. As both Ruffcorn and Klaiber acknowledge, that encounter may well occur in a variety of ways. Hence, evangelism needs to be defined more broadly than by the term "proclamation."

Evangelism as Entry into or Totality of the Christian Life?

One of the most crucial questions is whether evangelism is best construed as entry into the Christian life or as the totality of the Christian life. Most of the definitions contained in Mott's work relate to entry in one way or another.

But there is a significant group of persons who argue that evangelism (or evangelization, as they often refer to it) should be construed as everything the church does to bring the world into conformity with God's reign. Hence, in *The Second Wave: Hispanic Ministry and the Evangelization of Cultures*, Allen Figueroa Deck discusses evangelization as it applies to how God can bring an entire culture to comply more fully with God's will. Thus, justice, peace, prosperity, and other values can be se ism. However, Deck downplays the question of ho. are brought into the Christian life. This position is most plausible when one assumes that all the members of a culture are already Christian. If entry into the Christian life is through baptism, and all persons are baptized as a matter of course, then evangelism cannot be concerned with entry into the Christian life. Rather, it is the process of helping persons and their culture become sanctified or mature in their faith and life.

If evangelism is used as a reference for everything the church does, which admittedly aims at helping persons to become mature disciples, then there is no term given for the ministries that facilitate entry into the Christian life. As Christians come to deal with increasing secularization, even those with a commitment to the efficacy of sacramental initiation will admit that helping non-Christian persons become Christian is more and more a pressing priority.

Thus, whether the word "evangelism" is applied to the point of entry into the Christian life or something broader is a matter of usefulness. If it is applied to something broader, a new term needs to be found for ministries that deal with the entry point. It seems much more helpful to discuss discipleship as the broad aspect of how the church participates in God's mission of making disciples, while evangelism is that part of the mission that focuses on entry into discipleship.

Abraham's Definition

In my view, the best definition of evangelism offered so far comes from William J. Abraham. He says, "We can best improve our thinking on evangelism by conceiving it as that set of intentional activities which is governed by the goal of initiating people into the kingdom of God for the first time."[31] We have already examined in the previous chapter the reasons entry into the reign of God is an unsatisfactory way of defining this ministry. Rather, evangelism should be seen as initiating persons into Christian discipleship. Abraham is concerned that evangelism be seen as integrally linked with discipleship. His proposal for a new catechumenate is a helpful view about how initiation is best done, and it intimately links initiation with the rest of discipleship. His proposal is strengthened by my proposal for understanding evangelism as initiation into discipleship itself.

However, it is puzzling why Abraham limits the ministry of evangelism to initiating persons "for the first time." While he includes this in the first definition he gives, he does not argue for this aspect of it anywhere in his volume. When he explains initiation a few pages later, he says, "To be initiated into the rule of God is to encounter a transcendent reality that has entered history and to find oneself drawn up into the ultimate purposes of God for history and creation."[32] There are persons committed to the 1619 Synod of Dort's teaching that all of the saints are predestined to persevere to the end.[33] The modern version of that teaching is often summarized as "once saved, always saved." While Abraham clearly does not hold to this view, it is puzzling how he would treat the case of someone who had once been Christian but had then left the faith. When approaching a former Christian with the invitation to recommit to a life in Christ and re-enter Christian discipleship, why is this not evangelism? There are specific concerns that need to be addressed in such an encounter, including why the person left the faith in the first place. But such concerns are case-specific and are no different in kind from the many other specific concerns that each person brings as they consider entry into discipleship. Abraham offers no argument to support this position of restricting evangelism to the first entry. The phrase seems to cause many problems without offering any help in understanding the ministry of evangelism.

Evangelism Defined

My proposal is that we can best improve our thinking about evangelism by construing it as that set of loving, intentional activities governed by the goal of initiating persons into Christian discipleship in response to the reign of God.

Loving Activities

I have already argued that Abraham's definition does not adequately ground this ministry in the logically prior commandment to love God and to love one's neighbor as oneself. Far too often ministries called "evangelism" fail to love adequately the persons being evangelized. The question of what motivations people have for doing evangelism often renders evangelistic practice suspect and ineffectual.

Johannes van den Berg's discussion about the missionary motives of the Great Awakening in Great Britain provides a helpful list of motivations for mission. He lists political motives, humanitarian-cultural motives, the ascetic motive, the motive of debt, romantic motives, the theocentric motive, the motive of love and compassion, the ecclesiological motive, the eschatological motive, and the command of Christ as a missionary motive.[34] Many of these motives can be and have been construed in a variety of ways. However, by focusing on the motive of love and compassion, we find that the ministry of evangelism is both motivated and governed by the love that Christ commanded. By conflating 2 Corinthians 4:5 and 5:14, Charles Wesley brings the motivation for mission and evangelism to the fore.

> Freely to all ourselves we give,
>
> Constrained by Jesu's love to live
>
> The servants of mankind.[35]

It is out of love for others as whole persons that Christians engage in missionary activities, including evangelism. Christian love is grounded in God's love, and the love of Christ constrains—or in the words of the NRSV "urges us on"—to help transform the lives of others.

At the same time, love is the chief criterion for the adequacy of evangelism. When Christians commit unloving acts, they are not authentically evangelistic. They have betrayed the gospel and have profaned the name of the God they seek to serve. Love is not always judged by the perception of the recipient. Sometimes God's "yes" comes across as a perceived "no" by the person who is mired in sin and does not yet fully understand how God's word is really a saving word. Yet, the abuses of Christian evangelism have often claimed to be loving without fully considering the needs of the other persons.

I have argued that loving whole persons means meeting all of their needs. Thus, loving someone may require feeding them, housing them, or seeking to end the oppression that unjustly circumscribes their lives. At the same time, every person needs a saving relationship with Jesus Christ and to become a Christian disciple, participating in a Christian community. Thus, to feed someone without inviting them to become a Christian is to fail to love them fully. Conversely, to invite someone into Christian discipleship without attending to their social, political, and physical needs is to fail to love them fully.

Set of Loving, Intentional Activities Governed by the Goal

Evangelism is a ministry that takes many forms. It is not simply one activity, but a whole range of activities, all of which have the intention of initiating persons into Christian discipleship. Thus, while sharing one's faith with a friend and preaching are both easily seen as evangelism, so is mowing the church lawn. In each of these cases, the activity could be something other than evangelism. One can share one's faith to prove that one is superior to the friend. One can preach to reinforce that only those currently in the church will be saved and to reinforce the sense of being an elite remnant. One can mow the church lawn out of materialistic pride. At the same time, one can share one's faith as "one beggar telling another beggar where to get food."[36] One can preach the gospel to try to reach non-Christians with the message that God cares about them and seeks to have a relationship with them. One can mow the church lawn to show that Christians are persons who value beauty and have civic spirit. Such beauty and civic spirit may be prerequisites for some non-Christians to see the beauty of God's reign and the ways in which Christians contribute to the overall well-being of the community.

What is crucial in distinguishing all of these activities is the intention behind them. If the goal is to initiate persons into discipleship, it is evangelism. Whether the evangelism is appropriate to the context or effective is an important but secondary question. An evangelistic activity like preaching on street corners may work as it did for Wesley in the eighteenth century. One might view this method, if proposed for downtown New York City in 2002, as contextually inappropriate and ineffective. Yet, it is still evangelism. Sometimes one's judgments about appropriateness and effectiveness turn out to be mistaken.

Initiating Persons into Christian Discipleship

When construed as initiating persons into discipleship, the concern with how evangelism is connected with other ministries is cared for. Because discipleship has seven aspects (baptism, cognitive commitment, spiritual gifts, spiritual disciplines, conversion, morality, and faith-sharing), the life of discipleship is simply a continuation of each of these seven. When understood in this way, the relationship between evangelism and discipleship is like that of a foundation to the rest of the house. When the concrete slab is poured, the shape of the house is determined. How high the structure goes is a function of the plan of the structure and the time and the skill of the builders. But with a seven-sided foundation, the structure will presumably arise from each of the sides and the life of discipleship will take shape based on how the house was begun. Thus, in becoming disciples, persons move into a house that has a particular shape and their view of the world changes because of their new environment. There is a great deal to learn and explore once inside. One may enter the house through any one of the doors on the seven sides. Affirming the Nicene Creed may be the entry point for cognitive commitment, but seeking to understand the doctrine of the Trinity or the catholicity of the church is a life-long journey of study and intellectual growth. Faith-sharing may be exciting at first as the new Christian runs out to tell others, but over time the ability to share faith with others should improve. In time, each of the other aspects will provide ways in which the power of sin is diminished and the person's capacity to love God, self, and neighbor through worship, formation, and mission will increase. Moreover, all seven of the aspects interact with and reinforce each other since they are part of the same structure. The worship of God may lead the person to radical ministries of social justice, which may lead to faith-sharing with non-Christian persons, which may lead to a deeper understanding of one's cognitive commitments.

In Response to the Reign of God

Through all of this it has been crucial to emphasize that evangelism is not a purely human activity. As Paul said in 2 Corinthians 4:7, "We have this treasure in clay jars, so that it may be made clear that this extraordinary power belongs to God and does not come from us." Human beings are privileged to participate in God's saving acts. We do so as the church of Jesus Christ, and as individuals exercising our gifts to build up the church and participate in its mission.

Focusing evangelism on the reign of God does indeed remind us that God's purposes are the primary starting point for all of the church's mission, and that we sometimes seek to limit what God is doing to protect our cultural, material, and political privileges. We serve a God who is a God of justice, reconciliation, and peace, and who is going to save the world. Our ministries are in response to the saving activity of God.

PART II

The Practice of Evangelism

CHAPTER FIVE

Evangelism as Necessarily Enculturated

The New Understanding of Enculturation

During the two millennia of Christianity, the gospel has always been enculturated.[1] One of the hallmarks of Christianity is that it both is capable of being planted in different cultural contexts and in some ways requires that this be done. Before the self-conscious awareness of enculturation arose, the process had been going on for centuries. Dana Robert says:

> In addition to affirming the *missio Dei*, the Trinitarian basis for mission, missiologists in the 1990s are in nearly universal agreement that the gospel must be contextualized. The gospel takes shape from the local setting or else it cannot be understood by people in the particular culture. Fixing upon a balance between contextualization and remaining faithful to the core of the gospel is an ongoing issue in missiology.[2]

While the discovery of the importance of contextualization is relatively recent, the reality of this process in Christian history has always been present. Historically this goes back to the ministry of Jesus. Within the community of Israel, Jesus was continually breaking boundaries. Bosch says, "What amazes one again and again is the *inclusiveness* of Jesus' mission. It embraces both the poor and the rich, both the oppressed and the oppressor, both the sinners and the devout. His mission is one of dissolving alienation and breaking down walls of hostility, of crossing boundaries between individuals and groups."[3] Jesus reached out to women, to Samaritans, and to Gentiles in ways that surprised his followers and gave ammunition to his enemies. Following his death, the early Christian movement was open to the conversion of Gentiles, just as many in the Jewish community were. However, a breakthrough occurred in Antioch, where a new form of community emerged between Jewish and Gentile Christians. Bosch says:

> Even so, the Hellenists did not immediately launch a worldwide mission from Antioch. When it did come to that, it was Paul who became the catalytic factor. *He* was the one who provided the theological basis for the Torah-free self-definition of Gentile Christianity; it was his message that made the Christian *kerygma* intelligible and viable in the Mediterranean world and that prepared the way for a far-flung missionary program. Through the ministry of Paul and Barnabas the Antioch church became a community with a concern for people they had never met—people living on Cyprus, the mainland of Asia Minor, and elsewhere. They decided to send missionaries there . . . and went ahead and commissioned their two most gifted and experienced leaders to go (Acts 13:1f). This far-reaching decision and action was, however, not peripheral to the early Christian community, a kind of expendable extra. Rather, in retrospect it becomes clear "that Christianity had never been more itself, more consistent with Jesus and more evidently en route to its own future, than in the launching of the world mission."[4]

Christianity was thus translated from Palestinian Judaism to Hellenistic Judaism and ultimately to the Gentile world of the Roman Empire. This process is visible in the texts of the New Testament. The *logos* theology of John 1, used as a way of explaining the pre-existence of Christ, is only one such example. Bosch

examines how the conceptions of mission and the missionary prac-
tices of the church have changed in the variety of contexts in which
Christianity has been practiced. On this view, the practice of
Christianity among Presbyterians in Dallas, Texas, Pentecostal
Methodists in Chile, Greek Orthodox in Beit Sahour, Palestine,
Roman Catholics in Poland, Southern Baptists in Georgia,
Congregationalists in Massachusetts, and the Church of England in
Nigeria are all recognizably Christian, and yet they are working in
many different contexts and with many different forms and ways
of being Christian. Some of these differences can be accounted for
historically. Other differences arose because persons have sought to
enculturate the gospel in very diverse contexts.

Theological Basis in the Incarnation

There is a deep theological rationale for enculturation related to,
if not derived from, two essential claims of the Christian faith. First,
one of the most distinctive and fundamental doctrines of
Christianity is that the second person of the Trinity "became flesh
and lived among us" (John 1:14). In the words of the Nicene Creed,
"We believe in one Lord, Jesus Christ, the only Son of God . . . of
one Being with the Father; through him all things were made. For
us and for our salvation he came down from heaven, was incarnate
of the Holy Spirit and the Virgin Mary and became truly human."[5]
The doctrine of the incarnation teaches that God has acted to save
humanity by limiting Godself. Paul claims in Philippians 2:7 that
Christ "emptied himself, taking the form of a slave." God is greater
than could be seen in Jesus of Nazareth, yet, Jesus was truly God
and in him we see "God's glory." In John's view, whoever has seen
Jesus has seen the Father also (John 14:9). This idea of incarnating
the word of God has a strong connection to translating the gospel
into other forms as well. Andrew Walls has argued that

> incarnation is translation. When God in Christ became man,
> Divinity was translated into humanity, as though humanity were
> a receptor language. . . .
> The implications of this broaden if we take the Johannine sym-
> bol of the Word made flesh along with the Pauline symbol of the
> Second Adam, the Ephesian theme of the multi-ethnic New
> Humanity which reaches its full stature in Christ, and with Paul's

concern for Christ to be formed in the newly founded Gentile churches. It appears that Christ, God's translated speech, is re-translated from the Palestinian Jewish original. The words of the Great Commission require that the various nations are to be made disciples of Christ. In other words, national distinctives, the things that make out each nation, the shared consciousness and shared traditions, and shared mental processes and patterns of relationship, are within the scope of discipleship. Christ can become visible within the very things which constitute national-ity. The first divine act of translation into humanity thus gives rise to a constant succession of new translations. Christian diversity is the necessary product of the Incarnation.[6]

Since Christ is God put into human flesh, the gospel can be put into other languages and cultural forms.

The second theological argument is the universality of the mes-sage. God's love embraces everyone in the world, and God intends that all persons should be saved. Hence, the gospel needs to reach all persons where they are. The Bible can in principle be translated into other languages. There is a certain priority to the Hebrew, Aramaic, and Greek originals, but Christianity has from the begin-ning sought to use new languages and the concepts of new cultures to express the universality of its message. Universality does not require enculturation. Islam's universal message resists translation into other languages and cultural forms. To be read authentically the Qu'ran must be in Arabic. Universality combined with the doc-trine of incarnation points to enculturation as a necessary mission-ary strategy for Christianity. The historical precedents set by the first-century Christians made the choice for enculturation determi-native for the rest of the Christian mission. Arthur Kulah, an African bishop, puts this from his perspective, saying:

> The globalization of the gospel arises from an understanding and conviction that the Christian faith is truly a universal faith which requires the acceptance of a variety of cultural expressions while maintaining consistency with the theology and doctrines of the church. Incarnational theology includes contextualization or the attempt to witness to the gospel in radically changing economic, social, and political situations. Contextualization is not simply a matter of finding a new vocabulary. Contextualization is speak-ing the word of witness in the concrete socioeconomic and politi-cal context in which the church finds itself. The method of

contextualization will always seek the dialectical tension between *identity* (i.e., consistency with the confessed tradition) and *relevancy* (i.e., speaking the concrete word in the concrete context).[7]

Universality and incarnational theology combine to provide the theological rationale for translating the gospel into cultural forms that will carry Christianity's essential message to reach new persons.

Theological Basis in Anthropology

Every human being is a historical creature, living in a particular culture. Because Christianity is founded on God's love, and God's love embraces the whole person, then Christianity is required by its foundation to love the person's culture as well as the person.

This requires a careful negotiation as to what love requires. At one extreme, Christianity should not require that persons give up their traditional clothing patterns and begin wearing the suits and dresses of middle-class Americans and Europeans. Different types of clothing are compatible with Christian discipleship and should not be seen as something that should be changed. At the other extreme, some cultural practices are judged to be incompatible with discipleship. For example, ritual mutilation of young girls should be seen as violating the basic moral teachings of Christianity and for that reason avoided by Christian disciples.

Here even the New Testament is not always helpful because some of its practices are now widely seen as reflecting only a limited cultural perspective and not the universal teaching of the apostles. Women having long hair and slaves remaining slaves are examples of culturally bound practices that no longer apply. Other practices, such as the silence of women in church, contrast with more central and powerful claims in the New Testament that women are united with men in equality before Christ, an equality that ought to extend to church leadership.

The power of music is an important part of the Christian religion, and different cultures have developed widely different patterns of rhythm, melody, and harmony. Finding a way to praise God musically requires learning how to use the cultural resources that are present in a particular context to enable persons to praise God, to pray, and to hear God's word in ways that authentically connect them with God. Sometimes this means adapting music, poetry, literature, and other art forms already present in the culture. In other cases, it means gauging the people's capacity to learn new cultural forms and teaching them new music, art, and literature. New words may enable a burst of new, authentic worship.

The crucial point here is that the gospel has always been enculturated and must be translated if it is going to take root in new places and times. Mercy Oduyoye, says, "My position is that when the Good News comes to us in earthen vessels, we need to recognize the situation, break the vessels, and free the Good News. I often wished it were that simple. But if it were, we would not be keyed into the need to develop a theology of mission, which task demands that we clarify our terminology."[8] Oftentimes this is a long process whereby persons receive the gospel at first using the cultural forms brought by the missionaries, and eventually find their own voices and develop their own contributions to the whole church of Jesus Christ.

Understanding a Person's Context

Loving a person well means knowing as much as possible about that person. One must know their language and which dialect they speak. One must know the person's unspoken assumptions and patterns of social interaction. Questions about level and type of education, political and economic issues, views on nature and its patterns, musical and artistic tastes, employment histories, food preferences, competing religions, and all of the other factors that make up a person's culture, must be taken into consideration if one is to love a person well.

There are persons whose goal is to sell products to American consumers. They now gather data in a variety of ways, from taste-testing for certain foods, to focus groups, to cards that track a person's shopping patterns in grocery stores. They are studying their target audiences to understand them better in order to increase sales. Why is it that Christians do not study non-Christians with the same vigor as salespeople? If we are truly motivated by love and want to love others well, we need to be even better informed than those whose motives are less lofty. Hence, it is crucial that an evangelist use every tool available to learn about the persons he or she is trying to reach. Demographic studies, community data, and other collections of information can be extremely useful. But there is no substitute for simply spending time in the community and learning the cultural context that surrounds, supports, constrains, or shapes the lives of the persons one is trying to reach.

Starting Where a Person Is

Once that sort of study has been done, evangelism must begin where the person is. The successful evangelist will be like Paul on Mars Hill and look for ways in which God's grace has already been at work in the person's life. Sometimes this is done by connecting with a felt need that the person has. From a Christian perspective this felt need may be the first stirring of an awareness of a need for God. While the seeker may not express it that way, the Christian evangelist names it as such. For example, in modern American culture persons are often isolated because the contemporary culture has led persons to patterns that do not enhance community.[9] When persons begin looking for friends or a place where they might belong, they sometimes wonder if a church might be such a place. The seeker, in his or her own understanding, is not looking for God. But if Augustine is right,[10] his or her desire for community is really a restless heart seeking a relationship with God that can be found through the community of God's people—the church.

In a similar way, a person's educational level and language pattern should be considered when the gospel is presented. If one uses words learned in college to explain God's love to a person with a fourth-grade education, the message will not get through. Developing linguistic and cultural fluency so that one can communicate effectively is crucial to the evangelistic message.

Frequently, Christians are critical of the lifestyles of non-Christians and refuse to participate in the ways and visit the places where they might make friends with non-Christians and actually engage with them. Christians avoid bars because they do not value drunkenness or consuming alcoholic beverages at all. They do not walk the streets in dangerous parts of town or befriend junkies and gang members. Yet, they think abstractly that those persons need a relationship with Christ, and they wish that someone would find a way to tell them how bad off they are. George Hunter lists as one of his principles for an apostolic congregation that they "understand, like, and have compassion for lost, unchurched, pre-Christian people."[11]

Marketing Christianity?

In an important book, Philip Kenneson and James Street attack the ways in which marketing techniques are used by American congregations. They ask, "Put as starkly as we know how, the question is, Can the market-driven church remain Christ's church?"[12] They argue that church marketers believe the church's mission is to be a social service agency responding to the felt needs of persons. They say, "In short, we believe that adopting a marketing orientation runs the risk of transforming the church into a kind of community God never desired it to be. Perhaps more important, we believe that adopting a marketing orientation makes it less likely that the church will be able to fulfill its calling to be a sign, a foretaste and a herald of God's new creation."[13] What is at stake here is the theological judgment about the church's self-understanding and sense of mission. They attack George Barna, the pollster and church consultant, by saying he "no doubt believes that this image of the church's fundamental identity—the church is a service agency that exists to satisfy people's felt needs—is true to the character and mission of the church. We do not."[14] They conclude:

> Again, there is simply too much about the life of the church that will not fit this service agency mentality. For example, the heavy emphasis on felt needs all but drowns out the central teaching that the Christian life calls for a radical transformation and reorientation of one's whole way of thinking and behaving. Instead of assuming that membership in the Body of Christ entails far-reaching claims on our lives, church marketers assume that, at least in principle, the church can be made relevant and desirable to almost anyone if we simply know how to market it effectively.[15]

Kenneson and Street claim to have a passion for reaching unchurched persons, but this passion is obscured by the authors' other concerns.[16] Their contribution is clarity about the theological goals toward which the church should be moving persons. They document the blindness of marketers to ways marketing language corrupts the Christian faith. At the same time, Kenneson and Street are blind to ways in which theologically sophisticated language about the church being a "sign, a foretaste and a herald of God's new creation" blocks changes and adaptations to which the marketers point. Too often, church leaders believe that the way in which they came to experience Christ is precisely the way in which others should come to experience Christ. They have failed to wrestle with the variety of enculturations of Christianity throughout its history and to find a matrix for judging what truly belongs to the gospel and what is variable.

Yet Kenneson and Street make essential points. It is the gospel that is at stake. The church's calling is precisely as they suggest, and yet it is a calling to be a community of love that invites persons into the church as a response to the reign of God. How one balances the theological judgments about appropriate ways of manifesting the reign of God in a particular context is a difficult matter.

Homogeneous Units?

One of the most controversial ways in which the issue of God's calling for the church is pursued in a given context has to do with the homogeneous unit principle. Peter Wagner summarized Donald McGavran's missiological principle, discovered when the latter was a missionary in India. McGavran found that "people like to become Christians without crossing racial, linguistic, or class barriers."[17] McGavran defines his key term by saying, "The *homogeneous unit* is simply a section of society in which all the members have some characteristic in common."[18] There has been a storm of controversy over this idea, with many critics charging that it sanctifies and blesses racism, classism, and other forms of exclusion that are too often practiced in American culture. Kenneson and Street put the challenge precisely in terms of ecclesiology. They say, "A more disturbing problem with doing what comes naturally is that it encourages the creation and maintenance of homogeneous congregations. This is seen most clearly in the target marketing approach." Then they conclude,

> But to sanction the rebuilding of these [culturally segregated] walls in the name of attracting people is to forget who we have

been called to be. If the church is to be a sign, a foretaste, and a herald of a new humanity that God is bringing into being, a humanity in which the cultural barriers that matter in the world are torn down, then the church cannot, in the name of mission and outreach, encourage people to simply do what comes naturally.[19]

On their understanding the church must resist the urge to be with persons who are like the ones already there.

George Hunter makes the best case for how this church growth principle ought to be followed. He calls it "a case for the culturally relevant congregation."

> The largest and most widespread barrier (that we have any control over) that keeps people from faith is the culture barrier. . . . People phrase this barrier in many ways, but we can state its essence in one sentence: **They resist becoming Christians because they "don't want to become like church people"**— which they believe is a prerequisite for becoming a Christian. . . . Pre-Christians notice that church people have antiquated, or even foreign, tastes in music, art and architecture, that they love their traditions more than they love the surrounding community, and that they dress and act in "abnormal" ways. . . . We have thus rediscovered Donald McGavran's observation that the barriers that keep most people from faith and discipleship are more cultural and sociological than theological or religious.[20]

Here we have a clear disagreement about what causes persons to stay away from the Christian faith. Kenneson and Street say we are not distinctive enough in ways that make Christianity attractive as an alternative to a sick world. They say, "The real problem is not the strangeness of the church; people show themselves willing to wrestle with strangeness all the time. *The real problem is that unbelievers have so few reasons to endure the church's strangeness.*"[21] They suggest that Christianity is difficult and only by providing a clear alternative to contemporary culture will persons be attracted to discipleship. Hunter argues that the real barrier is that the church is strange in ways that are unimportant. When these cultural barriers are removed, the gospel is attractive and people are interested in coming.

Is it possible that both are partially right? The goal of Christian maturity is difficult, and Christians need to focus on faithfulness to God and God's reign. At the same time, the invitation to this way of life needs to be understandable if it is ever going to be perceived as a credible offer of God's love for a lost and hurting world. The way in which both of these positions can be construed as being right is to conceive of Christianity as a journey of discipleship. It must begin where persons are and strip away the nonessential barriers to the faith. Musical style is one such barrier, as is architecture. However, the gospel of including persons of all races and nationalities is an essential part of Christian teaching and practice, and it cannot be sacrificed.

When homogeneous units are culturally formed by ethnicity, language, and other factors, they can be a valid starting place for a Christian journey. But the character of the community must make it clear that new believers will be shaped in ways that will help them appreciate the diversity of God's people.

With regard to racism, for example, the congregation may be predominately of one race. However, it must genuinely welcome persons from other races if they choose to come. It should invite guest preachers and musicians from other racial groups. It should occasionally hold joint worship services with congregations that are from other racial groups in order to give visible expression to Christian unity across racial lines. It should set up study groups and social action ministries that are multiracial. At some point having a multiracial staff might be appropriate. Ideally each congregation will participate in larger ecclesial structures—conventions, dioceses, conferences, or other judicatories—that embody racial, cultural, and ethnic diversity. The catholicity of the church requires that each congregation manifest those inclusive relationships in significant ways in its life.

It is not necessary that every congregation be multicultural. However, given the prevalence of racism in American culture, it is necessary that each congregation become a tool for discipling persons to become the inclusive, loving persons God has called them to be. This means that explicitly racist practices are immediately condemned and the goals of inclusiveness and diversity pursued as much as possible.

Thus, the homogeneous unit principle is helpful when taken as an indication of where people are and how to connect the gospel to their lives. It is heretical if taken as a description of the goal of the reign of God.

Evangelism in Different Contexts

Evangelism is deeply relational. It begins with an invitation by someone who loves God enough to love another person so that there is a genuine invitation to the other to love God also. Because of this relational aspect of the ministry, evangelism in one context looks and feels very different from evangelism in other contexts. It will be suggested in the appendix that there are principles that underlie effective evangelism in every context. However, the implementation of these principles and the priority placed on various ones will vary from situation to situation. This judgment requires expertise on the part of lay and clergy leaders of evangelistically effective congregations. There is no substitute for knowing people. One must know their habits, their prejudices, their characteristic sins, their hopes, their social patterns, their economic status, how they interact with other groups, and many other factors.

The determination of context is a complex matter of judgment. Several possible factors could become significant: race, nationality, geography, ethnic group, economic class, level of education, language, immigrant status, and denominational affiliation might play a role. Their importance depends on which factors are regarded as most important by the persons one is trying to reach. For example, if a racial determination is thought to be most important, then a congregation might think all black persons will respond as a group. But black African immigrants might feel they have little in common with African Americans and would see themselves as more different than alike. Similarly, white residents of one town may view the white residents of another town as people who are very different from them. Economic class may bind together persons of many different races and ethnicities. The level of education might be more significant than immigrant status. Conversely, immigrant status might be more important than shared ethnicity, as when long-term Korean residents have little to do with newly arrived immigrants. The two following contextual descriptions, one based on geography and another on ethnicity, identify some relevant factors.

Evangelism in a Rural Context

Before my appointment as pastor of Prosper United Methodist Church, I had never lived in a small town. This was my first pastoral appointment, and I was the first full-time pastor for this congregation in more than forty years. The rural, Collin County, Texas, town had about one thousand residents; the church had forty-five in regular attendance. Prosper had no grocery stores, one café, a bank, and a good school system. Because the mail was not delivered to homes, one had to go to the post office to get it. While there were a few Hispanic families, most of the residents were euro-Americans with longtime roots in the community. Recently, a significant number of people had moved from nearby Dallas and the suburbs to the country around Prosper, disrupting the rhythms of the small town.

Little did I realize that this was, for me, a cross-cultural appointment, and it took me quite a while to understand that allowing only seven minutes for a trip to get the mail was a serious mistake. When going to the post office in Prosper, an effective evangelistic pastor should allow thirty to forty-five minutes. Six minutes will be spent driving there and back. The rest will be spent visiting with the postmaster, the persons waiting in line to be served, and everyone who comes in and out of the building's lobby. It took me less time to figure out that on Friday nights in the fall I was working. Attending football games was a mandatory pastoral and evangelistic activity. By attending the games, I met new persons, got acquainted with them and their families, and showed the community that I cared about what they loved.

I had been taught in seminary that one did pastoral counseling in one's office in fifty-minute sessions. No one taught me that in a rural context one normally did counseling with one foot on the back of a pickup truck in a parking lot or standing outside the school waiting for children. The conversations might last anywhere from six minutes to an hour. Further, my seminary education did not give me credibility as a counselor. Instead the trust that I earned during the first years of my service there led to deeper and more significant interactions during my last three years.

The image that everyone in a small Texas town is already Christian was ingrained in many person's minds. It was reflected in the speech patterns. People would ask "Which church do you attend?" The unspoken assumption was rarely rejected as inappropriate by the persons being asked. There usually was an answer, and if they didn't attend church it was regarded as a temporary matter that would soon be corrected. Yet, as I got to know the community, I discovered that most of the people were unchurched and that the community's self-image as a church-going community was inaccurate.

Prosper was a caring community that had several older residents who were important. It had several organizations that reflected the community's network of relationships. Most of all, it cared about its schools and the activities in which children and grandchildren were engaged. The three churches in the community were somewhat in competition with each other, but they managed to hold a joint Easter sunrise service and community breakfast each year. The absence of African American persons in the community was significant, but rarely discussed in the open. Like many rural churches, Prosper United Methodist Church was a warm, caring fellowship of persons that had shared the gospel with each other and their community for decades. There was a stable, deep sense of community that pervaded their life together. The choir was not large, but they loved singing.

Evangelism in a rural community like Prosper has a different shape and feel from evangelism in a rapidly growing suburb or an inner-city neighborhood. One older gentleman, when asked about someone in the community, would often say, "Oh, I've been knowin' him a long time." The relationship of these people to each other, to the land, and to the rhythms of agricultural life provided a depth that was important to them. At the same time, the influx of newcomers was creating a crisis as people had to cope with the beginnings of population growth.

Kevin Ruffcorn has had a much wider experience with rural congregations, and he notes many of these same strengths. At the same time, he analyzes weaknesses like poor self-image, isolation, and the idea that the pastor is the professional evangelist who is supposed to do the work for the laity.[22] Ruffcorn argues that small, rural churches can and should be evangelistically successful, but they need to understand what success looks like in their context. Many of the examples used in books written by pastors of mega-churches intimidate rural congregations. It is often too hard to discern principles, which are embedded in the numerical success stories, that might be helpful for a congregation struggling to keep the doors open. Yet there are evangelistically effective rural churches which, having analyzed their contexts well, effectively reach and disciple persons for Christ.

Evangelism with Hispanic Immigrants

One of the many lessons that persons engaging in ministry with Hispanic persons need to learn is that many Hispanics grow up thinking about God in ways that are markedly different from persons in other cultures. Luis Pedraja tells of the mistake made by persons who had not gained sufficient understanding of the context in which they sought to minister. He writes, "When well-meaning missionaries periodically came by the house to ask us if we knew Jesus, they were surprised when we would answer, 'Yes, he lives in that house across the street.' Unlike my English-speaking friends who considered it sacrilegious to name someone after God's Son, Hispanics consider it an honor and a constant reminder of God's nearness."[23] Pedraja then contends that this cultural context offers a perspective on Christology that helps the Christian community understand Christ more deeply.

> Because of the Incarnation, Christology also must contend with the historical realities of the world, including the suffering and oppression of the poor. Thus, the Incarnation forces theology and Christology to recognize that we do not live in a glorified world. Like Latin American theologians, Hispanic theologians also see Christ's suffering as continuing in the lives of the poor, the sick, the hungry, and the orphans of our world.[24]

Seeking to evangelize persons whose religious thought patterns are so deeply shaped by a sense of the nearness and humanity of Christ means adjusting the way the gospel is proclaimed so that persons may be reached and genuine evangelism may take place.

But there are also social patterns that are unique to Hispanic culture. First, one should realize that not all Hispanics are alike. Indeed, some prefer the nomenclature of Latino or Latina. Persons with cultural roots in Cuba, Puerto Rico, Mexico, Peru, San Salvador, and Chile often have different accents, traditions, foods, and approaches to key social issues. It does not take long to realize that Mexican Americans see themselves as different from Puerto Ricans who, in turn, see themselves as different from Cubans. Yet, in the ways they are treated by the dominant white culture in the United States, they have many similar experiences. Many of them speak Spanish, albeit with different dialects. Tensions between Spanish-speaking, bilingual, and English-speaking persons sometimes arise. Some Hispanics are recent immigrants still working through what it means to have left families and nations behind, while others are descendants of persons who settled in their state before it was part of the United States.

While many things are different in the various subcultures of the Hispanic community, one of the most common themes is the emphasis on family. Ruben Saenz says:

> The Hispanic community, by and large, is a relationship-based community; one enters into it and is accepted by the community often times only through introduction and by becoming familiar with the primary web of relationships of the individual doing the introducing. Once attaining access into the community, the patient ministry of presence is necessary to continue gaining the confidence and trust of a community. The ministry of presence can be exercised by attendance at family celebrations and/or other social settings without any particular agendas other than relationship building. Trust is greatly engendered with presence with someone undergoing a personal or family crisis. While this may seem like a lengthy way to go about the task of evangelism, it is a proven way to establish the foundation for building a community of faith.[25]

Saenz also argues that while ministry through family gatherings and small groups is key to evangelism among Hispanic immigrants, advocacy is also important. He writes:

> The Hispanic community, while soon to become the largest minority within the U.S., is virtually invisible. Its presence is

absent from the film industry, the television industry and society in general. With the exception of a few sports stars and entertainment icons the Hispanics are to be seen but not heard. This ethos of invisibility opens a door for exploitation and social marginalization.[26]

To ignore these issues that are so central to Hispanics while offering a relationship with Christ is to offer a partial gospel.

Common Themes in All Contexts

In the appendix, I will offer a systemic approach to congregational evangelism that is applicable to all contexts. How each of these should be implemented will vary from one context to another. What sort of media will work to communicate the gospel? An Internet website may be essential in one context and useless in another. Door-to-door visitations may be welcome in one community and deeply resented in another. Yet, it is all one gospel and it is possible to generalize some principles that underlie all of these practices.

Further, different contexts may cause certain components to receive a higher priority. In a community of poor immigrants, ministries of social justice might be of the highest priority while small groups for seekers are less important. In a suburban, middle-class context, the reverse might be true. Over time, however, both need attention in both contexts.

CHAPTER SIX

Evangelism and Ecclesiology

The Ecclesiological Implications of Evangelism

In earlier chapters I argued that evangelism is best understood as that set of loving, intentional activities governed by the goal of initiating persons into Christian discipleship in response to the reign of God. Further, I identified seven aspects of initiation into discipleship, one of which was the ecclesial aspect, and argued that Christian discipleship should always involve participation in a church and the means of grace that it supplies. However, the ecclesiological implications of this claim are complex enough that much more attention needs to be devoted to them. This claim requires that the persons carrying the ministry of evangelism must have a close relationship to a church. Ideally, it is the church itself that is doing the evangelizing, and part of the initiation process is the invitation to experience life in a local Christian community. Most of the time, initiation into the Christian life takes a long time. Frequently, it involves testing out worship, study, service, and other aspects of congregational life. Hence, if the congregation is part of the evangelistic process, then that part of the initiation process will happen naturally.

Over the last two centuries evangelism has often been undertaken by mission societies and parachurch organizations with a wide variety of relationships to churches. Some, like denominational mission boards, have a close working relationship with the rest of their churches. They tend to evangelize in the name of and on behalf of the congregations, judicatories, and/or bishops who will then welcome the new converts into that denomination. At the other extreme are parachurch organizations that deliberately avoid the discipline and responsibility of ecclesiastical involvement. When such organizations help someone become a Christian, there is sometimes little emphasis placed on helping persons find and become an active part of a congregation. The quality of the evangelistic ministry of such parachurch organizations, with respect to this component, depends on the quality and consistency of their support for churches with which they have relationships. To the extent that their evangelistic ministry does not incorporate new converts into congregations, they are failing to do evangelism well. To the extent that they are continually helping new persons become fully functional members of congregations, their evangelistic task is being accomplished.

The rationale for the existence of parachurch groups, whether they be campus ministries, revival ministries, crusade ministries, or mission societies, stems from failure of local churches to be evangelistic. Many congregations do not wish to reach out and offer the gospel to outsiders at all. They have become clubs existing for the benefit of their members. Other congregations do not wish to reach a particular population, such as students, immigrants, persons of a different race, or persons of a different social class. It is most frequently the case that a congregation will say they want to reach these persons with holistic, missionary ministry, but then they are unwilling to take the necessary steps required to realize their stated goal. Hence parachurch groups have emerged in part because of existing churches' failures to reach these groups of persons.

In actuality, the plethora of different churches formed in the United States during the last century is, in part, a reaction to this very phenomenon. Whenever a new group is not being evangelized by existing churches, the multidenominational ethos of Christianity in the United States both gives permission for and encourages the formation of a new church that will reach a specific group.

Looked at from the point of view of the person being evangelized, the ecclesial aspect of initiation into Christian discipleship requires that the individual find some congregation to join. Far too often, persons believe that being Christian is separable from belonging to a church. Frequently persons will say "I am a Christian, but I do not believe in organized religion." Statistics for most denominations in the United States suggest that the number of professing members is far greater than the number of persons who actually worship, study, or serve in those churches. For many congregations, it is common to have only 25 to 35 percent of their membership in attendance on any given Sunday, and even on Easter not all of the members come.

John Wesley faced this situation in a slightly different way in the eighteenth century. He argued against those he called "the mystics" who said they could be better Christians if they lived in solitude, away from the corrupting influences of others. To this Wesley responded:

> Directly opposite to this is the gospel of Christ. Solitary religion is not to be found there. "Holy solitaries" is a phrase no more consistent with the gospel than holy adulterers. The gospel of Christ knows of no religion, but social; no holiness but social holiness. . . .
>
> This then is the way: Walk ye in it, whosoever ye are, that have believed in his name. Ye know, "other foundation can no man lay than that which is laid, even Jesus Christ." Ye feel that by grace ye are saved through faith; saved from sin, by Christ "formed in your hearts"; and from fear by "his Spirit bearing witness with your spirit, that ye are the sons of God." Ye are taught of God, "not to forsake the assembling of yourselves together, as the manner of some is"; but to instruct, admonish, exhort, reprove, comfort, confirm, and every way "build up one another."[1]

Neither the mystic who thinks that a solitary life will conduce to holiness, nor the contemporary American who believes one can be a Christian without going to church has the Christianity of the New Testament. Wesley is right in linking the practice of New Testament

Christianity with participation in gathered communities. Those who claim to be Christian but have dropped out of the church or were never fully initiated into it thereby offer evidence that their claim is not true. To be a Christian disciple is to participate in a Christian congregation.

This then raises the question of what it means to "participate." Different Christian communities have different ways of identifying the practices that satisfy this description. Indeed, most communities would acknowledge levels of participation from adequate to exceptional. However, it might be agreed that regular worship, study, participation in the sacraments (however defined and however frequently offered), and accountability to the community are all aspects of this participation. It should be noted here that sometimes life circumstances prevent significant levels of participation. No one would challenge the Christian commitment of persons who are homebound because of illness or who otherwise spend their time serving Christ. Clearly the movement of many congregations to provide alternative ways of participating in worship, study, and service signal an intention to adjust to new cultural realities experienced by faithful Christians. At the same time, those who are able to participate and fail to do so call into question their Christian identity.

Evangelism Avoids Proselytism

One of the key words in my definition of evangelism is "initiate." This indicates the fact that evangelism is always aimed at those who are not Christian disciples. Proselytism is best understood as activities governed by the intention of convincing a Christian disciple to change membership from one church to another. If such actions are successful, there is no net gain for the reign of God because no new person has been added to the church of Christ. Instead, an existing Christian has been transferred from one part of Christ's Body to another part. In most cases this diminishes one congregation and enlarges another, but from the perspective of the mission of the church, there is no change. Hence, what is sometimes called transfer growth is illusory.

Beyond that, proselytism damages the church's mission because it weakens the common witness of the whole Christian church to non-Christians in their culture. If one group of Christians is seen attacking another group and attempting to steal their members, then non-Christians might be unimpressed at this body of persons who are called to love one another (John 15:12). When Christians are divided, then the world to which they bear witness about Christ has a harder time believing the gospel (John 17:20-21). The modern ecumenical movement has historically had a strong connection with the missionary movement in part because European and North American denominational differences were seen to be obstacles to genuine evangelism in other cultures.

Who Is a Christian?

The crucial question that must be answered if proselytism is to be avoided is who is a Christian? If evangelism is the ministry by which those who are not Christians are given a valid opportunity to enter into the Christian life, then it is important to know who such persons are.

Discipleship as Explicitly Faithful Obedience to God

In chapter 3 I argued that initiation into Christian discipleship has seven aspects. To be a disciple is to follow a way of life characterized by believing in Christ as expressed in all of those components. Such persons believe that God exists and loves them. They have experienced that love through conversion. They have responded by behaving in ways that are obedient to God's will. They have become part of the church through baptism. They receive the gifts given by the Holy Spirit. They participate with their sisters and brothers in the means of grace: worship, holy communion, Bible study, prayer, and service. They understand their whole lives as a form of witness, whereby they share their faith verbally and work to live lovingly and justly in the world. In short, Christian discipleship is a life of faithful obedience to God lived by persons who faithfully accept the call to discipleship.

NON-CHRISTIANS CAN BE SAVED

One must distinguish between discipleship and salvation. The question of whether persons who are not professing Christians may be saved is a notoriously difficult one. On the one hand John 14:6 says, "Jesus said to him, 'I am the way, and the truth, and the life. No one comes to the Father except through me.'" Similarly, Acts 4:12 has Peter proclaim, "There is salvation in no one else, for there is no other name under heaven given among mortals by which we must be saved." These texts have led some in the Christian tradition to proclaim that unless one explicitly professes faith in Christ in this life, one cannot enter eternal life.

On the other hand, some biblical texts suggest that all persons have received grace. Describing Christ, John 1:9 says "the true light, which enlightens everyone, was coming into the world." Theologically, the idea of God's condemning to eternal punishment persons who never had a valid opportunity to accept Christ as Savior contradicts God's attributes of justice and love.

My definition of evangelism is compatible with either of the positions described above because it does not equate evangelism with entry into the reign of God or into salvation. It focuses on entry into Christian discipleship. The next chapter will deal with the question of evangelizing persons from other religions and how this view would shape that kind of ministry.

DISCIPLESHIP AIMS AT CHRISTIAN MATURITY

The goal of salvation is Christian maturity.[2] What is essential to the Christian life is progress toward fulfilling the will of God. This is described in many ways, including maturity, perfection, having the mind which was in Christ Jesus, presenting one's body as a living sacrifice, sanctification, and being a holy nation.[3] Once discipleship is seen as a process aiming at this goal, then to be a Christian is to be one who is on that journey. Some of the texts in the New Testament speak of the Christian life as one would speak of running a race, or growing up, or being guided by the Spirit.[4] Thus, one does not have to claim to have reached the goal in order to be a Christian.

Inadequate Reasons for Claiming Christian Identity

Four inadequate reasons for assuming someone is a Christian are sometimes cited. Each of them has a relationship to Christianity as it should be practiced. All are partially adequate because of this relationship. Yet, when any one of the partial aspects of discipleship is raised to the level of sufficiency for Christian identity, then serious problems ensue.

NOT SELF-IDENTIFICATION

Christian identity is not based solely on one's self-identification as a Christian. Jesus said "Not everyone who says to me, 'Lord, Lord,' will enter the kingdom of heaven, but only the one who does the will of my Father in heaven" (Matt. 7:21). There may be pastoral reasons for taking someone's self-identification as a starting point for conversations about what it means to be a Christian and whether one's stated belief is matched with one's actions. Many persons doing evangelism in contexts where there are nominal Christians will often talk about what it means to be a real Christian. John Wesley and other leaders of the Evangelical Revival in eighteenth-century England were concerned at the wide gap between what they understood to be scriptural Christianity and the dominant patterns of Christian practice in their society.[5] In other places and times evangelists have sought to describe what it means to enter the Christian life and then to invite others to make the decision to do so on the grounds that they had not yet been real Christians.

Yet, the question of one's self-identification as a Christian has a role in discipleship because of the experiential aspect. Christians are those who believe in Christ, and part of believing is the conscious decision to place one's trust in him and accept his offer of salvation and incorporation into his Body. Thus, it is to be expected that Christians will have a self-understanding that they are indeed God's children. The problem comes in confusing the outcome of saving faith—one's self-identification as a child of God and disciple of Christ—with the criterion for becoming a Christian. We are saved by grace through faith, not by simply saying that we have done so.

NOT SACRAMENTAL HISTORY

Another reason often cited for ensuring Christian discipleship is the sacrament of baptism. Various doctrines of baptism are held among the various Christian churches, and some of these are interpreted to mean that in baptism God marks the person as one of God's children with a mark that is irrevocable. On this view, to be baptized is to become a Christian, to obtain a status that one can never lose. Thus, if a person was once baptized in a particular church, he or she remains a Christian disciple regardless of his or her later decisions or behaviors.

The practical implications of this ecclesiology are very important for evangelism, because many persons are baptized as infants or children and then do not practice their faith later in life. If evangelism is appropriately a ministry aimed at non-Christians, then such persons are not appropriate recipients of the evangelistic message. As Christians try to avoid proselytizing those associated with other churches, the issues get very sensitive indeed.

A practical example will help here. Assume a person was baptized as a Roman Catholic because he was born and raised in a Catholic culture where such behavior is the norm. He went through confirmation. Following that rite, he never worshiped regularly and never participated in the sacraments of the church as an adult. At age forty-five he emigrates to another country where United Methodist churches are active. A United Methodist asks him if he is part of a congregation and he says that he is not. She then asks if he would like to learn more about Jesus and think about recommitting his life to him, and he agrees. Eventually, he makes a profession of faith in Christ, joins the United Methodist church and identifies himself as a Christian. He experiences conversion, changes his immoral behavior, and begins active service to help the poor in his community find justice. He is now in worship every Sunday and receives the sacrament of holy communion regularly.

Have the United Methodists proselytized here? One Roman Catholic monsignor described this behavior as "sheep stealing." He said that the baptized person is part of the family and just because a person does not attend the family reunion does not exclude that person from the family. If the Protestant church wants to help that person, it should recognize that he is already a Christian by virtue of baptism and encourage him to return to active practice of the faith at his Roman Catholic parish church. However, a Roman Catholic archbishop who serves in a highly secularized part of the United States, when asked about the same scenario, told me that the United Methodists should invite him to become part of their church. There are far too many unchurched persons for one denomination to reach, he said, and if the United Methodists can reach him and get him worshiping, that will be a blessing to all concerned.

I am in agreement with the archbishop and not the monsignor. Baptism is an important part of the Christian journey, but it should not be seen as guaranteeing Christian identity. Many baptized persons drift away from the faith and even on their own understanding are no longer Christians. First Timothy 1:19-20 makes reference to Hymenaeus and Alexander who "have suffered shipwreck in the faith" and been turned over to Satan. Other examples of persons who once were Christian but have turned away from the active life of discipleship can easily be noted through Christian history and in present-day experience. To assume that all baptized persons are Christians is to mistake part of the journey for the whole of it. This was one of the accomplishments of the Evangelical Revival in England in the eighteenth century, where the Wesleys and others made a distinction between nominal Christianity and the real Christianity of faith, hope, and love. While Wesley believed in the sacrament of baptism and claimed never to have left the Church of England, at the same time he argued that persons should not assume that their baptism guaranteed them salvation or their status as Christians.[6]

NOT CHURCH MEMBERSHIP

Another way in which persons sometimes count who is a Christian and who is not is by formal membership in a Christian congregation. If their name is on the membership list of a Christian congregation, then they are identified as one of the members and thus as a Christian.

This approach would work if a Christian congregation exercised discipline over its members so that those who ceased practicing the faith were removed from membership. In reality, most congregations do not exercise that sort of discipline, and the relationship between church membership and practicing Christian discipleship is uncertain.

For example, I bought shoes at a store near my home and struck up a conversation with the saleswoman. She asked what I did and I responded that I was a United Methodist preacher. She told me that she was a Methodist as well and a member of a church in a town about two hundred miles east. I asked how long she had lived in this area and she responded ten years. I asked which church in this area she attended, and she said that she did not attend anywhere. I gave her the name and address of the United Methodist church closest to her home, but she indicated that she did not plan to attend.

The implications for evangelism here are clear. This woman is not a practicing Christian, and for any Christian group to offer her the gospel would be evangelism and not proselytism. If she has saving faith, there is a problem with how that faith is exercised, and the evangelist is giving her an invitation to Christian discipleship. In this case, the problem is that she claims to be a Christian but has not been attending corporate worship. It is probable that one or more of the other aspects of the Christian life—moral behavior, faith-sharing, cognitive commitments, sacraments, spiritual disciplines, and the exercise of spiritual gifts—may be lacking as well.

Not Geography or Ethnic Group

For centuries Christian identity was understood to be given by membership in one's community. To be born into medieval Europe was to be a Christian. Even at the end of the Reformation, the principle of *cuius regio, eiuis religio* applied—the religion of the prince determined the religion of the people that he ruled. Modernity and the diversity of religious choices has given many individuals in Europe and North America a wider spectrum of possibilities. Individualism as a philosophy has rendered the determinism of the community's religious identity less powerful.

Yet, there are still communities where one assumes the religious identity of the group. This is the Christendom model of Christianity where belonging to the group makes all the citizens of a particular country or community Christians. I was once part of a group that asked a leader of the Armenian Orthodox Church what percentage of the Armenian community were Christian. He looked at us as if the question were incomprehensible. Finally he answered, "Why, all of them, of course." We then asked what percentage of the community practice the faith and he responded, "About forty percent." It is clear that in some communities, merely being a part of the community means that one is a Christian by birthright.

There is a clear distinction that needs to be made between belonging to the community and practicing Christianity. Even if Christianity is the community's official religion or culturally dominant religion, getting the members of the community to practice the faith is important. Confusing Christian identity with membership in the community inevitably weakens the church, because compromises are made that tolerate persons believing they are Christians when they no longer live the life that Christians are called to live.

Implications of the Definition of Christian Discipleship

If Christian discipleship is understood to have seven aspects—morality, cognitive commitments, conversion, baptism, spiritual gifts, spiritual disciplines, and faith-sharing—it should be clear that their further definition is the appropriate doctrinal business of each Christian church. For example, the specifics of moral behavior appropriate to a particular Christian community may vary from one place to another because of the contextually determined issues at stake. Some communities may interpret Scripture's teaching about spiritual gifts differently from others, and the particular forms of service that are emphasized or required by a community may differ. Nevertheless, I am arguing that some form of practice in each of these areas is necessary to the fullness of the Christian life.

The difficulties come when faced with specific individuals and the question of whether that person is to be regarded as a Christian or not. It is probably not pastorally helpful to make too precise a definition as to what are the minimum requirements in each of these seven areas in order for a person to be a Christian. The question of how to regard someone who is fully engaged in two of the seven and minimally so in the other five is difficult at best. Further, how much of a commitment in each area is needed? What if a person is engaged in blatantly immoral behavior, yet still worships each Sunday, believes intellectually in the creeds, uses spiritual gifts, participates in the disciplines of spiritual formation, and volunteers each week as a counselor for the local homeless shelter? The difficulty of weighing such cases has led many persons to refuse to judge another person's status as a Christian.

Yet not to make some sort of judgment about the other person's status is to fail to love that person fully. If someone is hungry, homeless, or in need of clothing, it is obvious that the person is in need of help to safeguard his or her physical well-being. Similarly, if a person is not actively practicing the Christian faith in all seven of its aspects, it is equally obvious that there is a threat to his or her spiritual well-being. All other things being equal, it is better for a person to be a practicing Christian than not to be a practicing Christian. Loving neighbors means showing them how to be spiritually healthy and showing them where one has found resources to accomplish that goal.

Christians too often have led with condemnation and judgment. Whether it is missionaries who condemn indigenous religious practices or neighbors who tell their acquaintances that they are going to hell if they do not believe like they do, the condemnatory practices associated with some forms of evangelism have hurt the evangelistic task rather than assisted it.

Christians need to do two things simultaneously. They need to be clear about what the Christian life is all about. We cannot compromise on the good news of the gospel and its implications for one's life. They also need to invite others to join that life in a way that respects the other person's freedom to decide. If evangelism involves truly loving the other person, it must always have the character of invitation. It is an invitation for hearing the good news of God's judgment and God's offer of forgiveness and reconciliation.

Communal Validation of the Individual's Decision

Mere self-identification is insufficient. However, several of the seven aspects rely on self-identification. Only the individual can state his or her beliefs. One's Christian experience of conversion is likewise a matter for individual reporting. Some moral issues are a matter of individual sharing as well. Yet these aspects of the Christian life are routinely verified by the community in various ways. To join many churches a person must make a public profession of faith—that he or she believes in God and accepts the teaching of the Old and New Testaments. Some churches require completion of a catechumenate where the new Christian undergoes instruction and examination. Other churches call for public testimony of one's conversion experience both to validate the individual's status and to build up the rest of the community by example. Further, sharing about moral temptations and struggles is often a part of accountability groups in which Christians participate.

The rest of the aspects—morality, baptism, spiritual gifts, spiritual disciplines, and faith-sharing—are all subject to scrutiny by persons living in community together. If a person is not worshiping with the community, it is known by the others. If he or she does not participate in study, prayer, and other Christian formational disciplines, the community will know about that, too. A healthy Christian community will note such spiritual deficits and seek to help the brother or sister overcome them. This is Christian discipline aimed at healing spiritual wounds. Church discipline should punish spiritual transgressions only where such actions are intended to restore and heal. For healthy congregations, there is a communal dimension to the decision about who is a Christian.

The Church as a Means of Grace

The Christian life is one lived in the community of the church. This is deeply rooted in the understanding of the church as both a means of grace in itself and as the locus where God's grace is most consistently found. It is through the church that one's understanding of Christian doctrine is learned, elaborated, and tested. It is through the church that worship, corporate prayer, and the sacraments of baptism and communion are experienced. It is in the church that preaching of the gospel shapes one's life. It is in the church that opportunities for witness in both word and deed are continually offered and the challenges of Christian witness with the poor and marginalized are presented. Active participation in a Christian community is thus a key determiner in whether or not one should be regarded for evangelistic purposes as a Christian. Someone who is active in a Christian church and presumably making progress in the life of discipleship should not be evangelized. Someone who is self-identified as a Christian, baptized, and a member of an ethnic group that is presumably all Christian but is practicing none of the seven components, should be offered the gospel in an invitational way. This is not proselytism.

Recognizing Other Churches as Parts of the Church of Christ

This then raises the crucial question of which churches are recognized as authentic Christian churches? This ecumenical question has three implications for the ministry of evangelism. First, it shapes decisions about who should be evangelized. For too long Protestants and Catholics regarded adherents of the other side as non-Christians. Thus, missionary evangelism for Catholics was to go to Protestant countries and for Protestants it was to go to Catholic countries. Even within the Protestant sphere judgments were sometimes made that one church was the only church and all others were not "real Christians" because of some deficit in doctrine or practice.

The ecumenical movement made significant strides to repair this problem during the twentieth century. Through many years of dialogue, attempts at mutual understanding, shared ministry, and participation in organizations like the World Council of Churches, the Lausanne Covenant, and the National Association of Evangelicals, different church bodies have come to see each other as parts of the larger Body of Christ. Some denominations have taken official action to regard each other's members as Christians. The formation of Churches Uniting in Christ among nine of these denominations implies mutual recognition as Christian churches. The covenant relationship between the Protestant Episcopal Church in America and the Evangelical Lutheran Church carries the same implication and involves the mutual recognition of each other's ministries as well. More evangelical churches often rely on congregational decisions on such matters, but a noticeably more open attitude has been seen among them as well.

Such mutual recognition means that one should not evangelize persons who are active Christian disciples in those churches. But there are those who wish to be even more inclusive and refrain from evangelizing any body that calls itself Christian. Should Christians treat members of the Church of Jesus Christ of Latter-day Saints (LDS) as fellow members of the church? A Presbyterian answer is given in the following statement:

> The Church of Jesus Christ of Latter-day Saints is a new and emerging religion that expresses allegiance to Jesus Christ in terms used within the Christian tradition. It is not, however, within the historic apostolic tradition of the Christian Church of which the Presbyterian Church (U.S.A.) is a part. Persons of Mormon background intending to profess faith in Jesus Christ as Savior and Lord and become an active member of a congregation of the Presbyterian Church (U.S.A.) shall receive Christian baptism as administered by the Presbyterian Church (U.S.A.) or another church recognized as being within the historic apostolic tradition.[7]

In 2000 the United Methodist Church took a similar position, recommending "that following a period of catechesis (a time of intensive exploration and instruction in the Christian faith), such a convert should receive the sacrament of Christian baptism."[8] It also urges churches to use "Sacramental Faithfulness," a paper written prior to the UMC's General Conference that adopted this position. In that paper, the Reverends E. Brian and Jennifer L. Hare-Diggs explain that there are too many doctrinal differences for baptism in the Church of Jesus Christ of Latter-day Saints to be understood as Christian baptism. Such differences include the authority of Scripture and the LDS Church's inability to confess the Nicene and Apostles' Creeds.[9] There is thus a fundamental difference for a Presbyterian in approaching an active member of the United Church of Christ and approaching someone who is an active member of the Church of Jesus Christ of Latter-day Saints. The latter group of persons should be regarded in the same way as persons from non-Christian religions, a topic to be addressed in the next chapter.

Second, the ecumenical question pertains to decisions about whom we accept as partners in evangelistic ministry. Many times, evangelistic efforts are undertaken by more than one church at a time. Indeed, if all of a church's ministry has an evangelistic aspect, then anything that is done cooperatively by more than one church should have the character of joint evangelism. If an ecumenical food pantry is launched and the pantry's clients begin asking where to find spiritual food as well as food for their bodies, then the ecumenical group has engaged in evangelism together.

Care should be taken, then, in what partnerships are entered into by a church. Engaging in mission should be done only with those churches and groups with whom we can understand ourselves to be doing joint evangelization. Partnerships with others, such as secular governments, other religions, and those hostile to Christianity should be limited in scope and time or perhaps not entered into at all. Otherwise the evangelistic part of the missionary effort is limited because the partnership cannot accept that providing food, housing, or emergency relief might be done with the possibility that the recipient of the aid would come to faith in Christ through the encounter.

Third, are we prepared to help new converts join churches other than our own, and if so, which churches? Mission aims at bearing witness to the reign of God and not the aggrandizement of one's own particular church. Evangelism aims at inviting non-Christians to enter into Christian discipleship. It is necessary that the new believer become part of some church. But it is not necessary that the person respond by joining the evangelist's congregation. There may be valid pastoral reasons for the new believer to join a different denomination. This means that the evangelist must have an understanding of those denominations that it is acceptable to send persons to join. This is the practical, down-to-earth side of mutual recognition. If I believe that Roman Catholics are Christians, and the person who has just made a faith commitment would best serve God and grow in faith in a Roman Catholic church, then my job as a servant of the reign of God is to send that person to the nearest Catholic parish and help that person become a functioning part of that body.

This action does not preclude judgments about which denominations are better or worse in general or for particular persons. For example, I am committed to the ordination of women to the clergy and for equal participation of women in all levels of the church's life. Those Christian churches that limit women's roles are, in that respect, worse than the denominations that ordain women. Hence, I will be hesitant to encourage persons to join denominations that do not believe in this practice. However, I do not regard this as a church-dividing issue leading me to refuse to recognize those churches or send persons to join them. I will, however, discourage persons from joining them because I think there are better alternatives within the larger Body of Christ.

All of these give a special point to the ecumenical question of mutual recognition of churches. There are many things that divide the Body of Christ into different denominations. Some of the differences are grounded in doctrine. The question here is which doctrines are church-dividing? Clearly, for the Presbyterians, the question of being "within the historic apostolic tradition of the Christian Church" is determinative. For the United Methodist authors of "Sacramental Faithfulness," acceptance of biblical authority and confessing the historic creeds of the church is determinative. The LDS baptism question was settled on those grounds.

But what about the division between Protestants and Roman Catholics? Can Protestants recognize the Roman Catholic Church as a genuine church so that her members are seen to be genuine Christians practicing discipleship? If so, Protestants must avoid evangelizing practicing Catholics. Can the Roman Catholic Church see in Protestant churches enough of a churchly character to decide that evangelizing practicing Episcopalians, United Methodists, Presbyterians, and Southern Baptists is to be avoided? If so, they should avoid proselytizing Protestants.

Postmodern, Ecumenical Evangelism

In *Transforming Mission*, David Bosch argues that we are now moving toward a postmodern, ecumenical paradigm of the church. He believes that all of the ecumenical efforts of the last century "only make sense if they serve the *missio Dei*." Two of his seven points describing the unity of the church in mission are relevant to understanding the relationship of ecumenism and evangelism. He writes:

> First, the mutual coordination of mission and unity is *non-negotiable*. It is not simply derived from the new world situation or from changed circumstances, but from God's gift of unity in the one Body of Christ. . . .

> Second, holding onto both mission and unity and to both truth and unity *presupposes tension*. . . . Our goal is not a fellowship exempt from conflict, but one which is characterized by unity in reconciled diversity.[10]

Bosch is right in pointing to the emergence of an ecumenical paradigm for Christianity. The conflicts between Protestant and Catholic that ruptured Christianity in Western Europe are being seen in a new light.[11] The causes for many of the separations among Christian denominations that made sense when everyone was Christian are now being addressed. The Christian church finds itself facing cultures that are frequently either indifferent or hostile. In very few societies does Christianity hold a dominant place. Instead, postmodern, digital culture is more significantly influenced by secular forces over which Christianity has no control. In such an environment, minor disputes should not be allowed to cause major disruptions in the witness for Christ.

This situation has led to a rediscovery of the theological grounds of ecumenism and a reevaluation of the missional imperative it represents. It does not mean, however, that there is a new lease on life for the present shape of ecumenical organizations and relationships. Organizations such as the various councils of churches may or may not be the best way to express the missional unity of the church in the foreseeable future.

However, Bosch also castigates the formation of new denominations. He says,

> Fifth, if we accept the validity of mission-in-unity we cannot but take a stand against the *proliferation of new churches*, which are often formed on the basis of extremely questionable distinctions. This Protestant virus may no longer be tolerated as though it is the most natural thing in the world for a group of people to start their own church, which mirrors their foibles, fears, and suspicions, nurtures their prejudices, and makes them feel comfortable and relaxed.[12]

Bosch's critique is well founded but one-sided. What about tradition-bound denominations still living in the past who refuse to offer the gospel in terms that a new people can understand and accept? Their cultural imperialism often prevents new groups from coming to Christ because nonessential barriers such as language, clothing, music, and worship style are retained. Further, many churches have displayed little interest in evangelism at all, and then they are shocked when a new form of Christianity emerges that reaches people in new ways. Bosch's advocacy of unity-in-mission must apply to the ecumenically minded denominations who have placed evangelistic mission at the bottom of their priority list as well as mission-minded denominations who have placed ecumenical relations there. What is needed is a new form of ecumenism that places mission first and yet is very clear about building ecumenical relationships along the way.

The emerging paradigm will require an ecumenical attitude. This is due partly to the message of the gospel that Christian unity is a gift from God. But it is also due to the changed circumstances in which Christians find themselves.

Much of the current approach to Christianity was shaped by Christendom and modernism. As Christianity moves into a post-Christian and post-modern culture, it must once again see itself as a missionary entity. Mission is its reason for being. Authentic mission does in fact lead toward ecumenism, because it makes Christian witness more authentic. The way forward is to focus on mission and ecumenism simultaneously.

CHAPTER SEVEN

Evangelism and Persons from Other Religions

Questions about how Christians should view and relate to faithful adherents of other religions have been present since the first century. They became acute during the period of Christianity's missionary expansion. First came the question of whether Gentiles could be saved at all. Then, as Christians interacted with other persons in the Roman Empire and other areas of the world, Christianity's relationship to them had to be defined. The missionary expansion of Christianity from Europe to the Americas, Asia, and Africa forced Christian missionaries to address these issues more forcefully.[1]

As early as 1958, insightful theorists like Max Warren noted that the confrontation between Christianity and modern science would seem small compared with the coming confrontation between Christianity and other religions.[2] At the end of the twentieth century, two developments have rendered this issue even more critical. First, globalization has brought all the world's cultures closer together. Advances in technology and transportation have enabled more and more people to experience other cultures and other religions than the ones in which they were born. Increasingly, cultural patterns spread rapidly through globalized publishing of music and books. The Internet has further accelerated the diffusion of culture in ways never before seen.

Second, Europe and America, once regarded as predominantly Christian cultures, have become religiously multicultural. Since the Holocaust, Western culture has been forced to think differently about its Jewish citizens and their place in society. In recent years, large numbers of immigrants have come to the United States, Canada, and Europe bringing their own religious languages, traditions, and beliefs. No longer is the relationship with persons practicing religions other than Christianity and Judaism a matter only for missionaries in distant lands. In many places, relating to persons of other faiths is as close as one's fellow citizens. The various processes related to globalization mean that interaction between persons of different religions is increasing.

The nineteenth and twentieth centuries also witnessed the rise of a number of new religions, each of which poses interesting and unique challenges for Christianity. The Church of Jesus Christ of Latter-day Saints has spread rapidly to many different countries and to all fifty states. More recently, the Wiccan religion has gained accepted status, offering prayers at city council meetings and having their own chaplains in the United States armed forces. Many other religious groups have been formed as well.

Don Pittman, Ruben Habito, and Terry Muck offer an insightful introduction to their collection of readings about Christian attitudes and theologies about other religions. In *Ministry and Theology in Global Perspective*, they write, "The most widely employed typological distinction in the current debate among those concerned with developing an adequate Christian theology of religions is that which distinguishes between theological exclusivism, inclusivism, and pluralism."[3] They go on to suggest that this typology has both advantages and disadvantages.[4] In particular, there are a wide range of different positions that fall under each of these headings, and it is significant that in the variety of readings they offer, no one is labeled as fitting neatly under any one of these headings. Pitmann, Habito, and Muck characterize the first position by saying, "Those Christians whose positions may be identified with theological exclusivism firmly maintain that no salvation exists apart from the atoning action of the triune God known in the life, death, and resurrection of Jesus Christ and that no spiritual community other than the Christian church is a God-inspired mediator of saving grace."[5] While many variations of this view are noted, they continue,

> Theological exclusivists of all varieties emphasize that the Christian church is the sole religious community in the world with a legitimate missionary mandate. Personal evangelism tends to take precedence over other forms of mission because of the importance placed on profession of faith and obedience in baptism. The mission of the church is to proclaim Jesus Christ as Lord and, through word and deed, to convert the world to worship.[6]

Inclusivists, by contrast, include those persons who are willing to recognize that other religions *qua* religions are mediators of true grace. The authors describe this approach, saying:

> Characteristically emphasizing the *continuity* rather than the discontinuity between Christianity and other religions, theological inclusivists within the church have sought an appropriate way to affirm simultaneously the redeeming gifts and graces of God that may be operative in non-Christian religions as well as the finality of the revelation of God in Jesus Christ, which provides the criterion of every healing and saving process.[7]

According to these authors there is a third alternative:

> Pluralists have sought to articulate an even less ecclesiocentric and more theocentric Christian perspective. In accomplishing this they have focused attention on the relativity of all human knowledge, on the mutual sharing of religious experiences, and on the dialogical exploration in a multi-religious context of criteria for the discernment of truth. While remaining committed to Christ and the church, theological pluralists have asserted that such a commitment ought not imply either a pre-judged negation or diminution of other ways of ultimate transformation.[8]

Each of these positions is deeply connected to larger commitments related to epistemology and to theological views of revelation, salvation, and grace. Howard Mellor suggests that John Wesley was at the interface of the exclusivist and inclusivist positions,[9] and I want to argue that the theological commitments related to evangelism discussed in the previous chapters lead to the same result here. While a fully developed Christian theology of religions is beyond the scope of this brief chapter, how someone who shares my position might approach these crucial issues is worth exploring.

The Supremacy of Love as Motivation, Goal, and Method

The starting point for this understanding of evangelism is God's love of the world and God's desire for its salvation. God's mission is to save the world from sin and evil and to re-create it according to God's intention. John 3:16 affirms that God so loved the whole world that the Son was sent to save it and not to condemn it. Thus, any approach to non-Christians must begin with love. Christians have committed many evil actions against many different peoples in the last two millennia. Often, these actions have been done in the name of evangelism, conversion, mission, or another similar idea. One only needs to mention the Crusades, the Inquisition, the Conquistadors, or Christian participation in the slave trade, the Holocaust, or Apartheid to bring to mind historical events that tarnish the reputation of Christian relations with non-Christian peoples.

However, the record should also show that many Christian missionaries have endured great suffering and made significant sacrifices to bring good news and many types of assistance to newly encountered peoples. The conversion of many peoples, the founding of hospitals and schools, the healing of racial divisions, the ending of apartheid, the protection of indigenous cultures through the creation of written languages, and many other contributions to a tolerant and humane world have been assisted through Christian missions. The record of Christian missionary activities is a mixed one—neither totally evil nor totally beneficent.

It is clear that missionaries and evangelists have sometimes approached non-Christian persons with genuine love. Tolerance for others has been expressed in deeds of kindness and mutual respect while still making an invitation to Christian discipleship.

Regarding the relationship between evangelism and intolerance, Abraham makes the important point that any perceived connection is not a necessary one. He writes:

> Finding a correlation of sorts between some who believe in Jesus as uniquely revelatory and some who practice intolerance does not establish either a causal or logical link between the two. Intolerance has been fueled by many convictions and motives that have little to do with belief in the uniqueness of Jesus, and, even if it has been initiated by such belief, there is no reason why it may not be purged and overcome.[10]

He notes that, strictly speaking, intolerance is "a lack of respect for the beliefs and practices of others."[11] He continues, "Used loosely, it is extended to cover bigotry, narrow-mindedness, sectarianism, persecuting zeal, obstinacy, fanaticism, and the like. Understandably it also gets stretched to cover straightforward disagreement on important issues that are self-involving. This is the usage that is invoked when one applies it to those who hold to the finality of Jesus Christ."[12] Are Christian exclusivists necessarily intolerant? Abraham's careful analysis would indicate that any answer to this question depends on the meaning of "intolerant." Those who emphasize the finality of Christ do not necessarily lack respect for others' beliefs and practices. They may not and should not practice the kind of persecuting zeal that has too often been characterized by Christian efforts to evangelize. But they can be committed to the kind of disagreement that means that they do not accept the claims of other religions.

His arguments can be strengthened by the view of evangelism presented in this study. If evangelism is based primarily on God's universal love for all of humanity, it surely follows that such love includes respect for others' beliefs and practices. Truly loving others means knowing them and understanding who they are and why they live the way they do. It means understanding their culture and learning its internal logic so that its relation to the gospel of Jesus Christ can be made clear.

This understanding of tolerance is based on respect for the civil and human rights of others. One can be committed to a pluralist vision of the social order as the best and most loving way to deal with the plurality of peoples in the world while still being committed to the truth and superiority of one's own religious beliefs.

However, there is a further step that needs to be taken as a foundation for approaching persons of other religions. If love is the primary motivation and criterion of evangelism, then its practitioners should seek to understand other religions as carefully and objectively as possible. In a world where one's neighbors are likely to include Buddhists, Mormons, Muslims, Hindus, and Wiccans as well as Christians, it is important to know them well in order to love them well. That means understanding their religions as religions. This includes the doctrines, practices, and values of the religion with all of its regional variations. Such an understanding can contribute to a spirit of tolerance, allow for genuine dialogue, and pave the way for fruitful evangelism.

Universal Grace Is Prevenient

The universality of God's love is underlined by the many texts in Scripture that proclaim God's intention to save the whole world. Too often, Christians have had too small a view of God, thinking that God worked only in the ways to which we are accustomed.

The prologue to the Gospel of John puts the ministry of Christ in this larger perspective. By verse nineteen of chapter one, it is clear that Jesus of Nazareth is the main subject of the Gospel. But the chapter begins with the Word and acknowledges that the Word was God who was "in the beginning with God." Similarly, John the Baptist came to testify to "the light." Then, in a verse that is crucial for understanding how God's grace is universally given to all persons, the Gospel says, "The true light, which enlightens everyone, was coming into the world" (John 1:9). The implications of this text are clear. Somehow, the one whom we know as Jesus of Nazareth is also the Word of God, and this Word has a relationship with every person on the earth. The relationship is one of "enlightening" persons, since the Word is the "true light."

God's love is usually termed "grace" because it is given freely. The grace of God comes through the second person of the Trinity to all humanity. As I discussed in chapter 3, grace is given freely and comes before persons are aware of it or before they even seek it. Hence a number of theologians call this aspect of God's grace "prevenient," because it comes before other ways in which grace is experienced.

Implicit in the idea of prevenience is its universality. Precisely because this understanding says that God's grace comes before one's awareness of it and comes independently of the means of grace associated with the ministry of the church, grace is universal. It is given to all persons everywhere. This understanding of prevenient grace resonates with other texts in the New Testament that speak of Christ as bringing all things together. The Christ hymn in Colossians 1 says, "For in him all the fullness of God was pleased to dwell, and through him God was pleased to reconcile to himself all things, whether on earth or in heaven, by making peace through the blood of his cross" (Col. 1:19-20). Similarly, Philippians 2 envisions that God's exaltation of Christ will have a universal result. Paul says, "At the name of Jesus every knee should bend, in heaven and on earth and under the earth, and every tongue should confess that Jesus Christ is Lord, to the glory of God the Father" (Phil. 2:10-11). It is the desire of God that everyone be saved (1 Tim. 2:4).

This grace is universally given. In two key places, the book of Acts describes the apostles as proclaiming that God has reached out to the other nations with a measure of knowledge about God. In chapter 14 Paul and Barnabas are at Lystra. When they are mistaken for Zeus and Hermes, they address the crowd, testifying to the God who created the world. "In past generations he allowed all the nations to follow their own ways; yet he has not left himself without a witness in doing good—giving you rains from heaven and fruitful seasons and filling you with food and your hearts with joy" (Acts 14:16-17). In describing Paul's debate with the philosophers at Athens, the author of Acts takes a similarly broad approach to understanding God's work. A reference to their altar dedicated "to an unknown god" is the beginning point of one of his speeches. He said that God "allotted the times of their existence and the boundaries of the places where they would live, so that they would search for God and perhaps grope for him and find him—though indeed he is not far from each one of us" (Acts 17:26b-27). Other examples of Jesus' own practice indicate the ways in which he understood his mission as being first to the house of Israel, but then to the rest of the world. Bosch concludes that the boundary-breaking character of Jesus' ministry was a crucial component of all that he did.[13]

The Uniqueness and Finality of Christ

At the same time, other key texts of Scripture point to an understanding of God as a jealous God who will not tolerate the worship of other gods (Exod. 20:1-6). Howard Mellor argues that the texts of John 14:6 and Acts 4:12 are crucial for a scriptural understanding of other religions.[14] In the first of these, John describes Jesus as saying, "I am the way, and the truth, and the life. No one comes to the Father except through me." The latter text describes Peter and John speaking before the "rulers, elders and scribes" in Jerusalem. They are asked "By what power or by what name did you do this," referring to the healing of the man lame from birth. Peter concludes his answer by saying, "There is salvation in no one else, for there is no other name under heaven given among mortals by which we must be saved."

How are these diverse perspectives in Scripture to be reconciled? Many scholars will point to different authors and simply note the disagreements between them. Others will note that some communities, such as the ones that gave rise to the four Gospels, were struggling with distinct issues that pulled them in different ways. Thus the question of how to continue the mission to the Jews while at the same time opening up a mission to Gentiles led Matthew's community to shape a Gospel in which both concerns are expressed. The compilers of the Christian canon then placed four different Gospels side by side and understood that all of them bore witness to the same Lord and told the same truth.

Many of the problems in evangelistic practice have come from over-emphasizing one text of Scripture to the exclusion of others. A careful attention to the whole tenor of Scripture results in an unavoidable tension because of the many different voices and perspectives in the text. For our purposes, the tension present in Scripture can be summarized in five theses, all of which I wish to affirm:

1) God loves non-Christians.

2) God's grace is at work among non-Christians.

3) Non-Christians may be saved by Christ without explicitly confessing Christ as Savior.

4) Christians should love non-Christians as their primary duty.

5) Loving non-Christians should include evangelizing them.

The first two of these theses are amply demonstrated by the texts discussed above and are rarely disputed. However, the last three deserve more careful consideration.

Non-Christians May Be Saved by Christ Without Explicitly Confessing Christ as Savior

If God's prevenient grace is at work among non-Christians, then the question arises as to whether this is saving grace or not. God loves all persons and desires their salvation. Since God has elected all humanity for salvation, God's justice requires that they be judged on the basis of the grace they have received. Thus, if someone has never heard the gospel preached, then that person will presumably be judged on the basis of how God's grace came to that person and the degree of faith with which he or she responded.

As the inclusivists argue, it is possible to understand other religions as vehicles through which God has often worked. Because they teach doctrines and require practices that are contrary to Scripture, they cannot be judged as completely true. But in some cases they are best understood as not completely false, either. There are many ways of construing other religions as having strong connecting points with the gospel.

For evangelistic practice, this has been recognized by Christian missionaries who have used indigenous religious practices and adapted them to Christian purposes. Whether it is celebrating the birth of Christ on the Roman festival day of the Saturnalia, building a church on the spot formerly used by a pagan temple, or adopting rock music as a vehicle for Christian words, Christians have used both secular and religious practices of cultures as beginning points for communicating the gospel ever since Paul pointed to the altar in Athens. Some might argue that this is only a tactical maneuver with no further meaning or significance. However, it carries with it the implications that at least some aspects of other religions or of secular culture are either neutral with respect to the gospel or are ways in which God has prepared the way for the gospel to be heard.

Ultimately, any judgment about the salvation of any individual is left to God. It is God who knows human hearts and whether or not a person's faith is sufficient. For Christians to presume that they alone control the means of grace and that those from whom they withhold it are doomed to perish means that God's grace is no longer sovereign. William Temple puts this view very clearly, saying:

> So it may be truly said that the conscience of the heathen man is the voice of Christ within him—though muffled by his ignorance. All that is noble in the non-christian systems of thought, or conduct, or worship is the work of Christ upon them and within them. By the Word of God—that is to say, by Jesus Christ—Isaiah, and Plato, and Zoroaster, and Buddha, and Confucius conceived and uttered such truths as they declared. There is only one divine light; and every man in his measure is enlightened by it.[15]

This means that other religions are sometimes means of God's grace. The doctrine of Christ's finality means that in several important respects these religions are deficient, but in God's providence they function toward the purposes God has for everyone.

From this perspective comes the claim that when persons from other religions are saved, they are saved by Christ. George Lindbeck offers an interesting proposal in his *Nature of Christian Doctrine* when he suggests the possibility that some persons might be saved by a confrontation with Christ after death in which they recognize the best of their own religion and their own personal faith.[16]

Christians Should Love Non-Christians as Their Primary Duty

The understanding of God outlined in the previous chapters emphasizes God's love for humanity. Humanity's primary obligation is to love God with heart, soul, and mind. Loving God means loving all those whom God loves, and so Jesus says that the second great commandment is like the first—one must love one's neighbor. I have argued above that love of God and neighbor is the Christian's primary duty.

I have also argued that loving persons is a complex task that includes getting to know them and coming to understand their culture, their history, and their needs. While all persons are individuals, all persons also participate in social groups, and these interactions are complex because of the histories and larger contexts in which they take place. For example, when English-speaking Americans of European descent approach Muslims in Egypt, the interaction is more complicated than simply the feelings and thoughts of individuals. On each side, there are memories and associations of how Europe and, more recently, the United States have related to and treated predominantly Muslim Egypt for the last thousand years. Thus, when North Americans make casual reference to a crusade, they often mean a special effort to achieve a focused goal. When, after the September 11 attacks on the United States, President Bush used the word "crusade," most Americans could understand it in that light. However, Muslim Arabs hear the word "crusade" and immediately remember and think about the European armies attacking Jerusalem and other cities in the Holy Land in the eleventh, twelfth, and thirteenth centuries. In some Arab communities, stories of atrocities committed by the Crusaders have been linked to the perceived racism and economic oppression of colonial powers and now the cultural and military power of the United States. This linkage forms a particular understanding of Western culture in general and Christian Americans in particular.[17]

Imagine a young Egyptian Muslim man who holds this view of American Christians. The question for the Christian is "How do I best love this person?" This decision is determined in part by contextual factors and the specific realities of concrete situations. It is hard to imagine a genuinely loving response beginning with the demand that he convert to Christianity or go to hell. The priority of love would mean building relationships, looking at the world as he does, and explaining how one's Christian perspective is different from his and yet, in some respects, similar. This approach might take tangible forms such as providing education, medical care, and food. It might also take political forms such as standing with the poor and oppressed against the political domination of evil powers. Whatever it is that the person needs, love finds a way to meet those needs.

Loving Non-Christians Should Include Evangelizing Them

Loving whole persons includes attending to the spiritual aspect of their lives as well. Christians should respond to physical needs by feeding, housing, and clothing persons. During the twentieth century it became increasingly evident that Christians must also respond to the social and political needs of persons by pursuing justice for the oppressed. But the doctrine of the finality of Christ means that all persons would also benefit from an explicit relationship with Jesus Christ as Lord and Savior. This is true even for the most faithful adherents of other religions. I have acknowledged that such persons may have access to salvation. Their condition before God is a matter which we humans cannot judge adequately. While we do not rule out the possibility of their salvation, at the same time neither can we be sure of it. For the vast majority of persons, their relationship to God will be improved by entering into Christian discipleship.

God has called the church to be a primary means of grace through which the gospel is conveyed to the world. Preaching is a key activity. As Paul said:

> The scripture says, "No one who believes in him will be put to shame." For there is no distinction between Jew and Greek; the same Lord is Lord of all and is generous to all who call on him. For, "Everyone who calls on the name of the Lord shall be saved."
> But how are they to call on one in whom they have not believed? And how are they to believe in one of whom they have never heard? And how are they to hear without someone to proclaim him? And how are they to proclaim him unless they are sent? As it is written, "How beautiful are the feet of those who bring good news!" But not all have obeyed the good news; for Isaiah says, "Lord, who has believed our message?" So faith comes from what is heard, and what is heard comes through the word of Christ. (Rom. 10:11-17)

We have also seen that New Testament evangelism is more than just preaching and includes all forms of witness to the transforming love and power of God. However, the point here is that every non-Christian person would benefit from having a valid opportunity to receive Jesus Christ as Lord and Savior.

Loving other persons fully must include offering them an explicitly faithful relationship to Christ. Such an offer is not a violation of one's respect for them, nor should it ever be manipulative or coercive. Rather, this approach presumes that all human beings are beggars in search of spiritual food, and that we should share with fellow beggars the good news of where we have found food.[18]

The strongest objection to this position is based on the corruption of the Christian faith by Christians themselves. To some extent at least, every concrete expression of Christianity falls short of the gospel. Christians remain sinners, and the church, in each and every one of its denominations, is tainted by that sinful nature. Thus, in every ministry of evangelism there is always some imperfection. In some cases, invitations to Christian discipleship are made by individuals or by churches that have so fallen away from the gospel that the version of Christian discipleship being offered is hardly recognizable as such. An eighteenth-century bishop baptizing slaves *en masse* as they were led in chains onto boats for transportation to America is a clear example. Here there was no instruction in the faith, no sense of conversion, no inquiry into spiritual gifts or disciplines, and little in the way of Christian community. Thus, someone being offered this form of Christian discipleship might be properly led by God's grace to refuse the offer and to go on practicing his or her own religion.

While this is an extreme example, it raises the question of where one ought to draw the line. What if Christianity is so allied with powerful, colonial oppressors that the witness of Christians is not loving in any sense of the word? In such a case invitations to Christian discipleship would not be genuine invitations but versions so corrupt that God would surely excuse persons for refusing them. This underscores the importance of the word "valid" in David Bosch's definition of evangelism. He says evangelism offers "a valid opportunity to be directly challenged to a radical reorientation of their lives, a reorientation which involves such things as deliverance from slavery to the world and its powers."[19] Only God knows which opportunities are valid and which are not.

Again, the tension of preaching the gospel and evangelizing others is inescapable. On the one hand, in response to our own shortcomings, Christians are called continually to pursue reform in the church and in our own witness with the aim of being as faithful as possible to the gospel. On the other hand, we are always aware that we "have this treasure in clay jars, so that it may be made clear that this extraordinary power belongs to God and does not come from us" (2 Cor. 4:7). Genuine evangelism is done in humility, always seeking to admit the failings of the messenger and to keep the messenger from obscuring the message. But the messenger must not fail to deliver the message, however poorly it is done. In God's providence, when the gospel does move from one culture to the next, the new environment often adds new dimensions and strengthens its witness. This was clearly the case as Christianity entered the larger, Greek-speaking world of the Roman Empire in the first century. More recently, the development of Christianity in Africa, Asia, and Latin America has exposed political and other aspects of the gospel sometimes obscured in earlier versions.

While it is possible that there are some cases where the sinful failings of the messenger have so corrupted the message that evangelism should not take place, these cases are extreme and few in number. Paul says to the Philippians:

> Some proclaim Christ from envy and rivalry, but others from goodwill. These proclaim Christ out of love, knowing that I have been put here for the defense of the gospel; the others proclaim Christ out of selfish ambition, not sincerely but intending to increase my suffering in my imprisonment. What does it matter? Just this, that Christ is proclaimed in every way, whether out of false motives or true; and in that I rejoice. (Phil. 1:15-18a)

Christians should always aim at proclaiming the purest gospel in the most authentic way possible. At the same time, knowing that they fall short, they should trust that God will use their work and enable their proclamation to bear fruit despite problems in the way the seeds were planted.

The reason for evangelizing persons from other religions is that Christianity offers the grace of God in ways that Christians should understand to be more true, more complete, and more helpful than the ways that grace is made available in any other religion. Thus, all other things being equal, for a person to believe in Christ as Lord and Savior is an advantage for their salvation. While salvation is possible without such a conscious and explicit commitment to Christ, it is in almost every case harder without it. Just as persons seeking to cross a wilderness may in fact do so without a map, those who have maps should share their knowledge and even offer to guide those who do not. Authentic evangelism is only being done when one attends to all of its essential components.

Evangelizing Jews?

From the Christian perspective, the relationship between Christians and Jews is different from all other interreligious relationships. Christians should understand themselves as either originally Jewish or as Gentile Christians. The vast majority fall into the latter category, and so they should think of themselves as wild olive shoots grafted on to the rich root of the olive tree that is Israel (Rom. 11:17). Unfortunately, awareness of Christian dependence upon Judaism has been lost through Christianity's political and cultural domination of many of the Jews since the fourth century.

In a very perceptive and insightful essay Ellen Charry says, "It will be crucial to distinguish carefully between theological issues on the one hand and historical and pastoral issues on the other. While the former constitute the plumbline of the tradition, the latter are not to be taken lightly, particularly in this instance."[20] She recounts some of the historic changes in the "serious theological quarrel at the center of the Christian-Jewish argument."[21]

Charry's theological analysis of what it means to baptize a Jew highlights the special character of Jews for Christians. When pagans are baptized, they are welcomed into the household of God. But Jews have always lived there. Thus, to baptize Jews is to welcome them into the Body of Christ, but they are maintaining their lifelong relationship with the same God. Charry observes, "From this perspective, then, the body of Christ continues Israel's witness to God, now with Gentiles as equal partners. In terms of their relationship to God, nothing has essentially changed for Jews. In joining the body of Christ, Jews confess their understanding and support for God's gracious turn to the Gentiles."[22] Yet she argues that something dramatic has changed for the baptized Jew. While God's love for humanity and God's forgiveness and commitment to reconciliation is clear for Jews in their Scriptures, something new is added by Christian teaching.

> The story of God in Jesus is not the coming of God *to* us, for to this the history of Israel eloquently testifies; rather, in Jesus God comes *as* us, so precious are we to God. The gift of God in the cross is not the command of God to do God's will that we might live, but the humiliation of God that we might know the depth and breadth of love freely given, even unto death on a cross.[23]

Further, other truths are disclosed in this new Christian relationship for Jews. Charry says, "Advocates of a two-covenant theology who would deny that Jews need to know Jesus would deny them the deepest knowledge of God made known to humankind."[24]

Given this complex theological, historical, and psychological situation, she warns participants in the discussion against "facile recommendations."[25] She concludes her essay with the warning that dialogue will not work and that direct evangelism is ill-advised. She says,

> In short, the most constructive approach to the question of Jewish evangelism is, I think, to help Jews turn to God in their own language, liturgy, and symbols. While we believe that full knowledge of God is only known through Jesus and that the full stature of humanness is only perfected as his disciples, we must also acknowledge that most of us Christians are the wild branches that have been grafted onto the cultivated olive tree. Our confession of faith in God's Son is only as strong as the testimony of Amos, Isaiah, Jonah, and Ruth to the faithfulness of the God of Israel.
>
> Perhaps what we can learn from continued study of Scripture and history is that on this issue the way has not yet opened for us; therefore we are not permitted to proceed as if we were in control, for we are not in control. We should not withhold our own testimony from Jews interested in hearing it. But we do not know what God will do with that testimony in the life of that hearer of the gospel. . . . Faithful Christian witness is genuinely pastoral.

All we can do is trust that God is in control and confess our willfulness in wanting more vision than we are granted. We must wait upon the mystery of God's goodness, which we cannot see clearly in this case.[26]

Charry stands on solid, scriptural ground in her appeal to the "mystery of God's goodness." Paul says in Romans 11:25-26, "So that you may not claim to be wiser than you are, brothers and sisters, I want you to understand this mystery: a hardening has come upon part of Israel, until the full number of the Gentiles has come in. And so all Israel will be saved." Any Christian theology of evangelizing Jews must wrestle with Romans 9–11 and understand the limitations it puts on any easy solution to the issues that exist between the two groups.

As with all authentic evangelism, the priority is to love one's neighbor. Unfortunately, this has frequently been absent from Christians' attitudes toward Jews. Charry says:

> Under the banner of Christian love, Christians have oppressed and harassed Jews incessantly and in every conceivable circumstance. From a Jewish point of view, Christianity has little moral integrity. Ironically the Christian caricature of the hypocritical Pharisees is precisely the image Jews have of Christians. Based on Jewish experience, it is not clear that Christians take the Beatitudes seriously.[27]

Christians in America, along with Americans generally, often have very little historical consciousness about the context in which they seek to work. Hence, learning to love someone for whom the wounds of two millennia of Christian power are still raw is the first task before one speaks of Christ or conversion to Jews.

What Should Christians Do?

Given the foregoing analysis of theological issues and pastoral and historical situations, three conclusions are evident. First, any organized evangelistic effort to target Jews as a group in the present situation is unchristian. No Christian church or organization should engage in a special effort to convert Jews at any time in the foreseeable future. The history of Jewish-Christian relations requires repentance on the part of Christians as we contemplate the ways in which our theology has been anti-Semitic and our evangelistic practice has been racist and unloving.

Sometimes Americans resist thinking in terms of groups of persons, preferring to view individuals in isolation from their ethnic groups. But when a Christian church targets a group of persons for evangelism, then it is incumbent upon them to consider the relationships between the groups involved. The shadow of the Holocaust and the previous centuries of anti-Semitism loom large.

Seen in this light, any Christian church's organized campaign to convert Jews is highly problematic. By failing to understand the theological complexities of Romans 9–11, by failing to account for the centuries of Christian oppression of Jews—oppression that reached a climax in the Holocaust—and by failing to deal with the problem of anti-Semitism in American culture today, such a campaign would be both inappropriate and ineffective. It would be inappropriate because of its failure to love adequately the people it addresses. It would not seek to understand them or their deepest concerns and then to connect the gospel to their lives in an authentic way. It would be ineffective because the blunt instrument of a major campaign aimed at a group of people often marginalized in Western culture simply drives most of those persons farther from Christ by reinforcing the historic stereotypes of Christians as aggressive proselytizers and oppressors.

Bruce Marshall notes a commonly made proposal that Christians should reject the notion of supersessionism. By this he means that Christians should not believe "that the church has taken the place of the Jews as the elect people of God."[28] Marshall seeks to articulate a coherent position that is committed both to the permanent election of Israel and the unsurpassability of Jesus Christ. He says:

> If Christians can meet this challenge, the consequences for their theology and practice would be momentous. Christians would thereby grant that their own most central convictions not only permit but require them to regard the Jewish religion as willed by God to endure to the end of time, despite rejection of the gospel by virtually everybody who practices this religion. This would amount to regarding observant Jews not as practitioners of a dead religion, but as worshippers of the true God—and that not simply in the remote and elusive depths of their hearts (where, to be sure,

many modern theologians have wanted to say that all people do, or at least can, worship God), but in their public communal practice.[29]

Marshall leaves open the question of whether a mission to the Jews is permitted, let alone required. He appears skeptical of this possibility, saying, "Whether Paul or the New Testament as a whole permits, or even requires, the church to drop the idea of a mission to the Jews in view of their promised salvation remains in dispute, though even the most profoundly christocentric theologians have entertained doubts on this score."[30] Marshall's perspective provides a strong theological argument for respecting the status of Jews as God's elect.

At the same time, my second point is that any attempt to claim that Jews should never become Christians is not faithful to Christian discipleship. Because everyone needs to grow in their understanding and obedience to the truth, and because Jesus is "the way and the truth and the life," so Jews will benefit from learning "the truth that is in Jesus" (Eph. 4:21 NIV). Because Christians believe that Christ is the decisive revelation of God for humanity, they must offer this good news to everyone who does not believe in Christ. Paul, in his analysis in Romans 9–11, never lets go of the need for his kindred to be saved. He says, "For I could wish that I myself were accursed and cut off from Christ for the sake of my own people, my kindred according to the flesh" (Rom. 9:3). Later he says, "Brothers and sisters, my heart's desire and prayer to God for them is that they may be saved" (Rom. 10:1). David Bosch argues that Matthew's Gospel balances the continuing mission to the Jews by Matthew's predominantly Jewish community with the mission to the Gentiles. Both missions are related to each other and both require the other. Thus, for Christians to say that there is no longer any mission to the Jews at all is to violate some of the central teachings of Scripture.

Third, when loving and sensitive conversations and actions with individuals result in genuine evangelistic opportunities, Christians should actively pursue them and evangelize the Jewish persons involved. Consider the following situation. A forty-year-old Jewish man who was raised as an observant Jew and who went through all of the rituals prescribed by his Orthodox community comes to a Christian friend and asks about what Christians believe and how the Christian faith is practiced. The friend inquires and finds out that for twenty years the man was not religiously observant and that he has recently started a search to find a deeper relationship with God. He has gone back to the Orthodox synagogue and now has serious objections to its teachings. After trying Reform and Conservative congregations as well, he realizes that Judaism is not the path he wishes to pursue. Before investigating other religions, he comes to his most trusted Christian friend to see if Christianity is the true religion. How should the Christian respond?

This is one case where evangelizing a Jew is the appropriate Christian course of action. Such evangelization needs to be motivated by love and a deep understanding of this man's personal history and the meaning of his religious past. It must involve all seven aspects of authentic evangelism. At the same time, however, the process must respect the unique status that Jews have in God's plan for the salvation of the world.

Evangelizing Persons from Religions Other than Judaism

Adherents of non-Christian religions other than Judaism also need to be evangelized. Theologically speaking, they have a different status than do the Jews. When a Hindu becomes a Christian there is a different process than when a Jew becomes a baptized believer.

Yet, all human beings are also God's creatures, made in the image of God, and persons for whom Christ died. They are recipients of divine grace and in some measure enlightened by Christ before the first human evangelist ever approaches them.

For this reason, several of the things we have said about evangelizing Jews will apply to persons from other religions as well. The primary obligation is to love them. Understanding their history, their culture, and the ways in which God has already been at work in their lives is crucial. Building a relationship of mutual trust and concern is necessary for authentic evangelism. With regard to Muslims, for example, a great deal of improvement in mutual understanding is called for first. Edward Said's *Orientalism* is only one of many books which would indicate the ways in which Western attitudes toward persons from the Middle East affect aesthetic, scholarly, economic, sociological, historical, and philological texts.[31] Anyone trying to understand current geopolitical realities and their religious manifestations must get a handle on the centuries of relations between Christian Europe and America on the one hand and these other cultures on the other. Those who seek to evangelize Middle-Eastern Muslims have a lot to learn before genuine evangelism can take place.

Vincent Donovan's *Christianity Rediscovered* provides a moving account of how this might be done. Donovan abandoned typical missionary theory in an effort to evangelize the Masai in Kenya. He did not use a mission station to which the Masai were invited, complete with school, hospital, and chapel. Rather, he chose to go where they were and speak to them about the essential doctrines of Christianity in terms that made sense in their own culture. He demonstrated sacrificial love as well as a deep cultural understanding as he visited with them in their homelands. There can be no compromise on the essential doctrines of the gospel. But the long history of Christianity has shown the many different ways it can adapt to different cultural manifestations. In fact, the doctrine of the incarnation requires that Christianity be enculturated.

Thus, Christians have a mission to evangelize all nonbelievers, even those who are adherents of other religions. However, the commandment to love them takes priority and determines the way in which the evangelism is done. Once again, Christians should have a clear understanding of the cultural context in which they seek to serve. They must inquire about the relationships between their own country or culture and the one they seek to evangelize. Have Christians been oppressed there? Have they been respected members of the society? Have there been conflicts between Christians and persons from other religions? The success of Christian evangelization depends a great deal on the insights that the evangelist brings to his or her work with such persons.

Increasingly, we find those relationships within countries that formerly thought of themselves as Christian. In such settings there is often a religious competition among different groups, both to get a hearing and to gain adherents. In such a situation, Christians should participate fully in the marketplace of ideas. Just as Paul argued in Athens, so Christians should be a part of the cultural conversation in modern societies as well. Whether that is through the use of digital media in the United States, preaching in the open air in Malaysia, or offering Christ in a personal conversation with Hindu immigrants in the United Kingdom, Christian evangelism should take place.

However, all of the things said above about cultural and historical sensitivities with regard to Jewish persons applies as well to those from other cultures. In some cases the history of Christian oppression will be a negative factor, and organized Christian efforts at converting persons in a particular group will be wrong. In other cases, such as the Mormons, their institutional success has given them a level playing field and there is now possible a free and open debate for the hearts and minds of these persons in the United States. There is nothing wrong with a Christian church or organization planning to evangelize Mormons as a group.

Dialogue and Evangelism

One approach to interfaith relationships that has gained great respect in recent years is the path of dialogue. How should one understand the relationship between dialogue and evangelism? Are they compatible?

The word "dialogue" is sometimes used too broadly, covering all forms of interreligious relationships, and sometimes too narrowly, referring only to the interfaith efforts of official organizations like the World Council of Churches, the Vatican, or the World Jewish Congress. Instead, Edward Kessler says, "In reality, dialogue consists of a direct meeting of two people and involves a reciprocal exposing of the full religious consciousness of the one with the "Other." Dialogue speaks to the Other with a full respect of what the Other is and has to say."[32] Dialogue enables Christians to discover what God has done in other cultures. As the *Guidelines on Dialogue* of the World Council of Churches (WCC) says, it "is a fundamental part of Christian service within community."[33] This service has two types of results. First, the dialogue partners see that the Christians who proclaim a God of love are in fact exhibiting the kind of respect, tolerance, and desire for deep understanding of others that love requires. The willingness to enter into dialogue demonstrates love in action.

Second, the dialogue partners are also committed to hearing the Christian witness about God in depth. They give Christians the opportunity to explain the gospel in ways that would not be possible in a purely adversarial relationship. Thus, the WCC *Guidelines* says:

> Indeed, as Christians enter dialogue with their commitment to Jesus Christ, time and again the relationship of dialogue gives opportunity for authentic witness. Thus, to the member churches of the WCC we feel able with integrity to commend the way of dialogue as one in which Jesus Christ can be confessed in the world today; at the same time we feel able with integrity to assure our partners in dialogue that we come not as manipulators but as genuine fellow-pilgrims, to speak with them of what we believe God to have done in Jesus Christ who has gone before us, but whom we seek to meet anew in dialogue.[34]

It is precisely this last point that causes concern within Christian circles. The evangelist is the bearer of good news from God. If the messenger does not believe in the truth of the message, why deliver it? If the evangelists are "genuine fellow pilgrims," then dialogue seems to presuppose a pluralist approach that says all religions are equal.

William J. Abraham, too, argues that dialogue and evangelism are categorically different. He says:

> What is absolutely crucial to dialogue is that those engaged in it respect the beliefs of those who share in the process, and that they be prepared to follow the conversation and the evidence wherever they lead them. The latter claim is implicit in the act of dialogue, for if one is not prepared to change one's mind in the light of what is presented in conversation, then one is not really taking the partner in conversation seriously.[35]

He says dialogue serves many good purposes and is worth pursuing for its own sake.

Abraham then gives a mixed conclusion. On the one hand he says that dialogue should not be used as "a covert form of evangelism." On the other hand, he says that if that is avoided, "there is no reason why Christians who are also committed to the task of evangelism may not engage in dialogue with integrity."[36]

Abraham's apparent contradiction is truly only apparent, and it is best seen in confronting a false dichotomy contained in the WCC

Guidelines. The last sentence in the WCC statement quoted above juxtaposes "manipulation" and "genuine fellow pilgrims," as if there were a simple choice between the two possible approaches. Abraham juxtaposes "covert forms of evangelism" with genuine dialogue.

There is a third alternative to both dichotomies. It is an approach that presumes that one's basic commitments are correct, but that they can and should be enhanced by engagement with others. Further, it openly and honestly says that dialogue is worth pursuing as a form of evangelism. As long as this is stated candidly at the beginning of the dialogue process, there should be no problem with each side proceeding. Indeed, in dialogues between two missionary religions like Islam and Christianity, each side should presume that honest representatives of the other side would always have as part of their agenda the conversion of the other. Kenneth Cracknell, a Christian scholar who has spent much of his life engaged in interfaith dialogues, said, "Dialogue is evangelism and evangelism is dialogue."[37] Insofar as the truth is what we seek, we are genuine fellow pilgrims. But Christians who have received the revelation of God in the Scriptures know the truth, and thus, they approach dialogue with the attitude of faith seeking deeper understanding.

The reason the World Council of Churches' statement and Abraham can both affirm dialogue and evangelism is that Christians who know the truth recognize that they may know it only partially. The essential doctrines of the faith are not at risk. Yet, so much more of God and God's work in the world can be known and learned through dialogue. Dialogue can be transformative in the sense that encounters with other religions can cause Christians to understand their own faith more deeply and to rediscover aspects of their tradition that have been forgotten. In every instance, the practices of other religions are to be measured by the gospel of Christ, but that is not the same thing as measuring them by the current practices of a particular community of Christians. Christian churches often distort the gospel, and it is sometimes through dialogue with other religions that they are called to rediscover their own best practices.

The Importance of Interreligious Cooperation as a Form of Evangelism

Christians must play three roles simultaneously. First, we must act as neighbors to those practicing other religions. We must love them and care about their well-being. Most Christians have become convinced that religious toleration is a necessary part of any valid political system today. This means the government must protect the freedom of its citizens to practice religion in any way they wish, as well as the freedom to change religions as they so choose. Thus, when the religious freedom of Mormons, Muslims, Jews, or those of any other religion are threatened, the Christian obligation is to act politically to protect freedom of religion. Being good neighbors also includes providing appropriate hospitality and inclusion in civic functions. Second, Christians may find opportunities for cooperation with persons from other religions. There are a number of issues on which religious people can agree and where cooperation will enhance rather than restrict Christian witness. For example, Pittman, Habito, and Muck make an eloquent plea for interfaith cooperation on issues that face the world today such as world peace, the environment, and racism.[38] Third, we must act as witnesses, never forgetting that we are called to "make disciples of all nations" (Matt. 28:19). There is inescapable tension among the three roles. While others may not see the connections that Christians see, nevertheless Christians must do all three simultaneously.

A Systemic Approach to Congregational Evangelism

Evangelism can be done through a variety of organizations and agencies. I have argued that authentic evangelism must maintain the closest possible connection to a local congregation in order to facilitate authentic initiation into Christian discipleship. Hence, the ideal situation is for the congregation itself to be the evangelistic organization. But how does one create an evangelistically effective congregation? The first step is to clear away a number of misconceptions regarding how evangelism should be practiced.

Correcting Misconceptions

Numerous misconceptions about evangelism are held by laity and clergy alike. While many of them have a grain of truth contained in them, all of them militate against clear understandings of the church's task in this area. Some of these misconceptions are included in the literature about evangelism and infect many of the programs and ideas currently being proposed to local congregations. Yet, the theological commitments regarding evangelism described in the previous chapters will correct many of these misconceptions. Some of the most popular, including a brief reminder of what is wrong with them, are as follows:

Misconception #1. Evangelism is primarily about saving the institution through getting new members, preferably those who tithe. Too many church leaders are preoccupied with institutional maintenance, forgetting that the church lives and dies by its faithfulness to its mission. Church growth and financial health are results of effective evangelism, but they should not be the primary goal.

Misconception #2. Evangelism and missions are two separate activities, best cared for by different committees. Mission describes everything that the church does for those outside itself, and almost everything it does has a missional component since outsiders are often participants in its activities. Evangelism is an essential component of mission. Separating mission and evangelism misconstrues what they are. Assigning them to a committee as if the other activities of the church are not missional or evangelistic is inaccurate as well. Every committee of the church should have the mission of the church, including its evangelistic component, at the forefront of its thinking.

Misconception #3. Evangelism is something optional that we do when we get around to it. Evangelism is central to the gospel and is never optional.

Misconception #4. Evangelism and social action are opposed to each other. In pursuing one, you exclude the other. Evangelism is a way of inviting persons to participate in God's coming and present reign of justice, including social justice. Social action is a way of demonstrating the present reality of that reign in a way that invites both the oppressors and the oppressed to join.

Misconception #5. Evangelism is the pastor's job; don't ask or expect laity to do it. Laity are usually more effective evangelists than pastors. It is the pastor's job to empower the laity to be evangelists. However, to empower them the pastor must also model evangelism personally. The main point of the pastor's work is to hold up the vision of a missionary church engaged in evangelism and then provide training and systems that enable laypersons to initiate others into Christian discipleship.

Misconception #6. Large, suburban, upper-middle-class congregations are the primary places pastors should go to learn how to build successful congregations. Many such congregations are models from whom principles and practices can be learned. At the same time, each congregation must learn how to be evangelistically effective in its own context and with the resources it currently has. Many small congregations serving poor, urban, and rural communities are also evangelistically effective, and we need to use them as models as well.

Misconception #7. Television, radio, and other digital media necessarily distort the gospel and should not be used for its communication. Digital media have their limitations, which must be recognized. They are often impersonal and limit the message to a sound bite. At the same time, their vast reach and their acceptance by modern cultures means that they are inescapable tools for communicating the gospel. But they are not sufficient in and of themselves.

Misconception #8. We need to evangelize immigrants in order to help them become good Americans. All non-Christian persons need to be evangelized. However, many immigrants are already Christians, and they need invitations to join congregations as baptized sisters and brothers. The goal of evangelism is not to make persons into good citizens, but to help them become what God wants them to be. Evangelism that is motivated and guided by love will be much more sensitive to asking about the real needs of all sorts of persons. Paying attention to immigrants is a good thing provided that it is done out of love.

Misconception #9. Crusades, revivals, and the ministries of parachurch organizations are the best examples of evangelistic practice. Churches tend to glorify the practices of the past. Someone once said that the seven last words of the church are "We've always done it that way before." It is my view that while these practices have some usefulness, effective congregational evangelism is far more important.

Misconception #10. We have too many churches already, we are short of clergy, and we don't need to start new congregations. Churches that lose their sense of mission usually die. Other churches are affected by population shifts. Many denominations have too many congregations in areas where they once had vital ministry but where there are far fewer people today. At the same time, as new cities are built and new ethnic groups arrive, most denominations should be rapidly starting new congregations aimed at building up new communities of faith.

Missionary Ecclesiology

The second step in the congregational practice of evangelism is emphasizing that the church is a missionary organization. Far too many congregations and Christian denominations see themselves as clubs operating for the benefit of their members. William Temple is quoted as saying, "The church is the only society in the world which exists for the sake of those who are not members of it."[1] Sadly, this is far from true in many places. A consumer mind-set has set in where people join churches asking how they can benefit from what the church offers. Mature Christians come to church asking how God can use them to make a difference in the world.

The difference in a congregation's decision-making process can be decisive. A missionary church composed primarily of persons over the age of sixty hires a children's minister to reach out to immigrant children in the neighborhood. A club church hires a senior citizens' ministry coordinator. A missionary church sets its budget so that half of its offering goes to serve the poor through programs that feed them spiritually and physically. A club church spends money to remodel the sanctuary so that the color scheme is fashionable. A missionary church is continually praying for guidance about unreached persons with whom they can share the gospel. A club church is busy making sure that only persons who are like them are admitted into membership. A missionary church is willing to adapt its methods to reach new persons with the gospel. A club church is jealous of its operating patterns and resists change at all costs.

Missionary Leadership

How does one develop a deeply rooted sense of mission? Like the old joke about the three determiners of a home's value (location, location, location), the three determiners of how a congregation becomes missionary are leadership, leadership, and leadership. The development of missionary leaders, both clergy and laity, is the third step in practicing congregational evangelism. A congregation with missionary lay leaders will help make the decisions needed. Missionary congregations are engaged in continually giving away their resources for the benefit of others. Such sacrificial giving goes against the selfish interests that are endemic in modern culture, and so it is a continual struggle to give away as much ministry as we can. Key lay leaders in a congregation must continually stand up and remind their brothers and sisters that Christ talked about losing one's life for Christ's sake as the way to find it (see Matt. 10:39). The paradox is that churches that focus inwardly die and missional churches thrive. The role of clergy leadership varies from one denomination to another and also from one size congregation to another. However, the ministry of preaching and teaching is primarily lodged in the clergy, and those are two key functions in helping focus the congregation's identity on its mission. If the clergy are in charge of ordering the church's life (i.e., making programmatic, staffing, and financial decisions) then their visionary leadership in these areas is crucial as well.

Vision is crucial for any human organization. The vision of what God is doing in the world and how that congregation is called to participate in God's mission is crucial for determining everything else that it does. The leadership of the church must make a conscious decision for the church to be evangelistic. A congregation's intentional decision to be evangelistic is the most important decision in the process. Such a decision must involve the clear understanding about the changes that have to be made to truly embody that intention and the costs that will have to be paid to be successful. Making that kind of decision requires leadership from both clergy and laity.

Analyzing the Congregation as a System

A crucial corollary to the understanding of evangelism presented in this book is that evangelism involves a wide range of different activities. When they are lovingly undertaken with the intention of initiating persons into Christian discipleship, these activities are evangelistic. The fourth step in practicing congregational evangelism is envisioning how all of these activities are interrelated.

A very important approach to human organization comes from the business community. Peter Senge and others have long advocated taking a systems approach to the analysis of a business. In *The Fifth Discipline*, Senge recounted the playing of a simulation game where beer is being distributed. While each person is doing his or her job well, but focusing only on his or her job, a developing problem is not noticed by anyone until the business fails. He also recounts the competitive advantage a Japanese automaker had over a Detroit one. In the American-made car three engineers had been involved in the engine's design, and they specified three different bolts, requiring the assembly line to stock those different parts and use three different wrenches for them. Instead, the Japanese company had looked at the whole engine and realized the savings of time and money that could come from using the same size bolt.[2] Senge advocates what he calls "systems thinking," which is "a discipline for seeing wholes. It is a framework for seeing interrelationships rather than things, for seeing patterns of change rather than static 'snapshots.'"[3] Someone in leadership must look at the whole and see the many ways the different parts shape and relate to the other parts.

For a congregation, evangelistic effectiveness is a function of many different parts, all of which are interrelated. The list of twenty components that follows could be outlined in a number of different ways. However, the underlying idea is that mission, hospitality, and invitation are important ways of thinking about the whole system of the congregation's ministry in this area. The missional components—numbers 1, 2, 3, and 4—are the most important. If these are in place, the rest is just details. However, leaders must pay attention to all of the factors. There is no single program, idea, or emphasis that can make a congregation evangelistically effective. Because evangelism is essentially relational, and because relationships are multifaceted, a congregation needs to be doing all these different things at once. Excellence in one area depends on and also reinforces excellence in other areas.

The hospitality and invitational components—that is, components five through twenty—should be seen as comprising a possible or typical journey from being an unchurched or pre-Christian person to being a committed, growing disciple of Jesus Christ. Clearly, not everyone follows these steps in the same order, and some of them may not apply to a particular seeker's experience. However, a congregation's system of evangelism must be ready to offer each step to persons when they are ready to take them. While not all individuals will do all of them or do them in order, having all of them operating effectively will mean that the congregation's overall ministry is sound.

Twenty Components

1. Create and Sustain a Missional Culture

How does a congregation become a missionary body? The most important way in which this is done is through the internal communication of the gospel. Mission is first of all God's mission, and the congregation seeks the privilege of participating in that mission. Thus, it is crucial to know what God is doing in the world and how the congregation can best participate in God's work.

Preaching must focus on God's saving activity and how human beings are called to respond to it. Over time the sermons should shape the missional ethos of the congregation by continually reminding them of how God is calling them to give of themselves for the sake of the world. Sermons should change individuals. But they should also change congregations. A church that has continually heard the missionary gospel preached over several years will most likely take one of two courses of action. They will either respond and become a missionary congregation, or they will find a way to get a new preacher.

Similarly, there should be biblical and doctrinal teaching that shapes the congregational ethos for mission. Bible study groups should be engaging the Scriptures to learn how God is working in the world today. Richard and Julia Wilke's *Disciple: Becoming Disciples Through Bible Study* is one such study that combines scholarly understandings of the biblical world with conversation about what discipleship today truly means. The last part of each of the thirty-four weekly sessions asks about "The Marks of Discipleship" and how the individual is going to respond to the

Scripture by living differently. This kind of Bible study shapes the people into a missionary congregation.

Another crucial tool for this component is the development and use of a mission statement. Richard Warren's *Purpose Driven Church* gives clear guidance about how the statement ought to be developed. It should be grounded in Scripture and owned by the whole congregation. Ideally, the congregation will spend six months in Bible study seeking to discern God's will for the church. After summarizing the findings of the study in writing, the congregation should distill it down to a single sentence. Warren says that a good one will be biblical, specific, transferable, and measurable.[4] The statement should be brief enough to be memorable and yet deep enough to support sustained conversation and discussion about how best to implement it.

The church's mission statement should then be used in a variety of ways. Warren's "Nehemiah Principle" suggests that "vision and purpose must be restated every twenty-eight days to keep the church moving in the right direction."[5] This is a shallow and mechanical approach to how the statement ought to be used. Rather, a deeper approach would require the leadership of the church to be continually communicating the vision in multiple ways. It ought to be communicated regularly in sermons, in the worship bulletin, in church newsletters, on bulletin boards in the hallways, in worship, and at the start of committee meetings. It ought to so pervade the life of the church that two things happen. First, every member of the congregation ought to be able to repeat the mission statement. It should shape their understandings of who the congregation is and what it is trying to accomplish. When someone joins the church they ought to be aware that they are joining a community whose purpose is to fulfill the mission as expressed in this statement.

Second, every decision taken by groups in the church ought to be tested against the mission. Some possible courses of action are contrary to the mission of the church. Racially based membership requirements would violate the church's commitment to offer the gospel to the whole world and to embody the diversity of God's people. Operating an antique business out of the congregation's education building might not be contrary to the mission, but it might be utterly unrelated to it.

Other decisions have to be prioritized according to how well or how poorly they support the mission. Those tasks that are closest to the heart of the mission ought to receive the greatest amount of support in the use of staff, lay members, facilities, and money. Thus, a Vacation Bible School that reaches all of the children in the community ought to have higher priority over the men's fellowship group that has not had a new member for twenty years. These are difficult decisions, but referring to the mission statement can provide the right context in which leaders can make sacrificial decisions.

2. Create and Sustain a Spiritual Culture

The church should understand that salvation is by God's grace and that whatever ministry is done in evangelism is done as a part of God's action in the world. Evangelism done on the basis of cultural superiority or religious manipulation is not true evangelism. Rather, in humble acceptance of what God has done and is doing, evangelism must participate in that larger divine mission. This deep sense of humility and reliance on God in the ministry of salvation is necessary to make sure that evangelism does not get corrupted by other impulses. Too often Christians have presumed that their form of Christianity—enmeshed as it is in their cultural trappings, their methods of education, and their economic systems—must be the way in which others receive the gospel.

If there is a deep spiritual awareness that God is the source of the process and that all others are recipients of God's grace, then a different attitude can exist. One practice that serves this goal is for the congregation to have an organized, sustained prayer ministry that focuses on intercession for pre-Christians. The church should understand that it is relying on God's action and that it is being used by God as a means of grace. Prayer changes the world and those praying for the world. It acknowledges that God is the one at work in this process. Through prayer, we are both asking God to reach specific persons and offering ourselves to God for direction in that process.

Part of fostering a spiritual culture is the basic doctrinal understanding of the community. There must be theological commitments evident among the clergy and lay leadership of the congregation that are compatible with evangelism. For example, some commitments to universal salvation lead to a lack of interest in inviting others to become Christians. If one believes that all other religious commitments, so long as they are sincerely held, will lead to salvation, then offering an opportunity for commitment to Christ can be viewed as a culturally imperialist way of denying the validity of other religions. On this view, religious dialogue and mutual understanding are the most important things, and attempts at converting persons from another faith to Christianity are seen as disrupting the mutual tolerance and respect necessary for life in the modern world. Adherents of this view might claim that, because no one can truly know the truth or falsity of any religion, all religions are equally valid. Since God is a God of love and God wills all persons to be saved, then universal salvation means that our efforts at offering the gospel to others are more likely to do harm than good.

In a culture where pluralism prevails and religious commitments are seen as private preferences, this theological view will tend to undermine the effective ministry of evangelism. Instead, evangelism is strengthened by the view that, all other things being equal, the life of a non-Christian person is enhanced by making a commitment to Christ. The idea that this has some connection to salvation and that being a Christian is a better way of life leads the evangelist to offer the gospel to the non-Christian person as an act of love.

3. Create and Sustain a Culture of Hospitality

One of the key features of Jesus' ministry was the boundary-breaking approach of his preaching of the reign of God. He ate with tax collectors, spoke with Samaritans, praised the faith of Gentiles, and continually reached out to the lost ones of Israel. Thus, when the apostolic church accepted Gentiles on the basis of faith and not obedience to the ceremonial law, this was truly faithful to the mission that Jesus had already put in place. Paul's proclamation of the gospel made it clear: "For in Christ Jesus you are all children of God through faith. As many of you as were baptized into Christ have clothed yourselves with Christ. There is no longer Jew or

Greek, there is no longer slave or free, there is no longer male and female; for all of you are one in Christ Jesus" (Gal. 3:26-28).

The gospel is intended to reach all persons everywhere. It is intended to cross all boundaries, including race, age, nationality, gender, and other cultural factors. It is a universal gospel intended for every human being.

While almost all Christians would accept the universality of the gospel and embrace the racial and cultural diversity of the whole church of Jesus Christ, the question is whether each congregation ought to mirror the diversity that will exist within the reign of God when it comes in its fullness. Stephen Rhodes makes an excellent argument that this diversity is actually God's will. Rhodes continues by arguing that each congregation should reflect the diversity of its community and be as multicultural as possible.[6] Faithfulness to the gospel requires that each congregation must, in both word and deed, offer genuine hospitality to all persons. When a church is predominantly Anglo and an Hispanic person seeks to join, that individual should be fully welcomed. When a church full of wealthy persons has a homeless person attending, that person should be fully welcomed.

Given that most Christians still hold prejudices on the basis of race, economic class, marital status, age, education levels, and other factors, it is crucial that the congregation confess its sins in these areas and make sure that it is inclusive of every person that it can reach. Each congregation should examine its practice and its current demographic makeup, and determine how it can reach new groups of people to add to those it is already reaching. Despite one's best research and planning, however, there are always surprises. Consequently, a missional congregation is always ready for the unexpected. Hebrews 13:2 says, "Do not neglect to show hospitality to strangers, for by doing that some have entertained angels without knowing it."

4. Determine Your Target Population and Learn to Love Them Well

Given each congregation's social and cultural location and their limited resources of personnel and money, a congregation must focus its resources on a particular target population. By necessity, targeting one group will mean giving less attention to another group for the present, but successfully reaching one group will often create opportunities to reach other groups later.

The church's leaders must make a clear decision about who the target population is. This could be defined by age, family structure, geography, income, race, immigrant status, or other cultural factors. It will be influenced by the group(s) that the congregation is already reaching and the possibilities for connecting with other groups from that base. The congregation's leadership must study this population so that they know the group's culture, its thought patterns, its needs, its hopes, and how the gospel might most readily be communicated to its members. The leadership should lead the congregation to love the members of that group as well.

5. Demonstrate Concern for Physical Needs and Justice Issues in the Community

The congregation as a whole, and especially identified leaders of the congregation, need to be active in the justice issues and physical needs of persons in the community they are trying to reach. Love must be concrete, and it should embrace the whole person. This includes political issues where the Christian faith has a specific position to advocate.

Food banks, medical and legal clinics, employment services, community organization, political activism, community development, and other aspects of community involvement may all demonstrate the love of Christ to people. Attending to the poor and marginalized is especially important because of the strong connection between the reign of God and justice for the oppressed.

There must be a constantly maintained connection between ministry to physical needs and ministry to spiritual needs. Simply having a food pantry is insufficient. Instead, the pantry should be in a strong relationship with the people it is serving so that the church can determine the long-term causes of their need and the appropriate long-term solutions. Part of the solution is ensuring that such persons are given an opportunity for embracing the gospel and becoming Christians. Hence, it is fully appropriate to follow the example of one Christian food pantry where a staff person frequently calls for quiet and then prays fervently and out loud for all of the people in the pantry at that time. A ministry to the homeless should not only include counseling and food, but it should offer opportunities for worship and community as well.

6. Empower Laity to Witness Verbally to Their Friends, Associates, Relatives, and Neighbors

All laypersons should understand themselves to be verbal witnesses for Christ. They are more often in contact with pre-Christian and unchurched persons, and they are frequently more effective witnesses than clergy.

Witness can be categorized into three levels. The simplest level is to talk about one's faith and Christian activities when the subjects naturally come up in conversation, and follow that with an invitation to attend church if they do not already have a church home. A second level is to tell one's own story about one's relationship with God. A third level is to invite non-Christian persons to make commitments to Christ and to lead them through the process by which those decisions are made.[7]

7. Achieve Visibility Among Your Target Population

For a congregation to be known as a place where persons can find what they are seeking, it has to achieve visibility within the culture. The best way of achieving this kind of reputation is by the verbal witness of its members. Within the target population, the church should strive to be known as a place where love is shared, God's grace can be experienced, and the deepest of human needs can be met. The church's witness for justice and the physical needs of the people will help achieve this visibility.

Visibility alone is insufficient. The church must be known in ways that positively represent the gospel in the larger society. It should be known as a place of inclusion and acceptance rather than exclusion. It should be known as a place of love rather than hatred and division. It should be known as a place where people are cared for rather than rejected.

In many cultures, the location and appearance of church buildings can be an effective way for unchurched persons to know that you exist. Facilities should be clean and well-kept according to the community's standards. Artwork and architecture should carry spiritual messages that will be understood by non-Christian persons.

In many areas, this visibility will also require some sort of advertising. While the next component addresses how the evangelistic message is communicated, the methods described there also raise the visibility of the church as the message is being communicated.

8. Use an Appropriate Communication System to Invite Persons to Know Christ

Once the target population has been determined, then the congregation must ask what communication systems are most effective in reaching that group of persons. Because of the personal, relational nature of the gospel, face-to-face, one-on-one communication will normally be best. That is the reason that every congregation must rely on the verbal witness of its laity among their friends, relatives, associates, and neighbors. However, each group of persons will also have more general ways in which to communicate the gospel. In some communities, it may be signs on the bulletin board of the laundromat. In other places, hand-written notices stapled to telephone poles will work. In other communities, direct mail will be the best way to communicate.

In most American contexts, it is important that congregations use electronic media to reach persons outside the church. The dominance of television, radio, and the Internet as patterns of communication is clear. Every congregation should find ways to use televised worship, advertising and news stories to communicate its message. In some areas, radio may be a cost-effective way to reach a target audience. More and more churches are using websites as a way of communicating with those who want to know more about its message and its ministries. How e-mail and electronic bulletin boards can be used to reach the unchurched is not yet clear, but there is great potential here. It was argued above that the gospel must be enculturated. Just as Christians used books during the first few centuries of its mission, and just as the Protestants rapidly adapted to the invention of printing with moveable type, Christians today must adapt to the dominant modes of communication in a digital age.[8]

9. *Provide Adequate Parking, Signage, and Facilities*

Hospitality means welcoming the stranger in ways that he or she will understand and appreciate. In some contexts, that means helping persons find the church from a bus stop or subway. But in many other contexts, persons will drive to church in an automobile. There, adequate parking facilities that meet cultural standards are necessary. In many parts of the United States, the cultural standard is now that an organization should offer off-street, paved parking within sight of the building's front door. Some cultural patterns will mean an average of only one and one-half persons per car. In such contexts a congregation that wants to be hospitable to 450 persons needs 300 parking spaces.

Whatever the context, the question is how best to help non-Christians feel welcome as they arrive at the church building. Congregations that pay particular attention to this aspect have teams of greeters who help persons park their cars. When parking conditions are crowded, the leadership of the church should be the ones who deliberately take the worst parking places and leave the ones closest to the door for visitors.

What happens to the first-time visitor when they approach the building? There should be adequate signage to help them find where they need to go. Families with children, may need to locate the nursery. The location of restrooms should be made obvious. Signs pointing to the worship space (whether it is called the sanctuary or something else), should be clearly visible. For some churches, an information booth is staffed by persons who can give directions. Even then, signs need to direct persons to the information booth. Signs for the church office would be helpful during the week.

The building's architectural features should convey the spirit of hospitality. Simply by looking at the facilities everyone should feel welcome. The building ought to meet the highest standards of accessibility for disabled persons. Posters, decorations, and even the color of paint used should make for a welcoming environment as perceived by the persons the church is trying to reach. The sanctuary or worship space should not appear to be full to the first-time visitor. In many places, full is defined as anything over 80 percent of capacity because at that level, visitors will perceive that there is no room left for them.

10. Welcome Visitors with Demonstrated Hospitality Measured by Perception of Visitors

When the first-time visitor walks into the building, he or she should be greeted by someone who is genuinely interested in helping them. This means that the church must cover every possible entrance. Greeters need to be sensitive enough to discern those who are first-time visitors and would welcome special attention. It is helpful if there is an information booth or other means of helping visitors feel comfortable and find what they need. This point of contact is the first of four opportunities to get names, addresses, telephone numbers, and e-mail addresses. The others are Sunday school, registration during worship, and conversation after the worship service.

Following the worship service, laity should intentionally seek out visitors and welcome them. Church leaders should model this for everyone else by making sure that they do not spend the first few minutes after the close of the service speaking to persons they already know. Instead, it should be their job to introduce themselves to someone they do not know. This enables persons either to meet a new brother or sister in the church, or to offer genuine hospitality to a newcomer.

11. Have an Effective Nursery/Children's/Youth Ministry

Parents care deeply about their children's welfare and how they are treated. Your nursery should be brightly colored, inviting, safe, and well staffed with the same trusted people each week. Your nursery's adequacy should be evaluated periodically by a committee of young mothers. Make ministry with children and youth a priority in your congregation's programming. Enlist the best, most spiritually mature leaders in the congregation for this ministry.

12. Worship Indigenously

The three most important factors for creating indigenous worship are music, music, and music. Other key factors include the pace and sense of formality of the service and the content of the sermon. The bulletin should be user-friendly for pre-Christians (e.g., print out the Lord's Prayer). The criterion of true worship is not whether the congregation has always done it that way, but whether the liturgy enables the people to worship God authentically.

13. Get Names, Addresses, Telephone Numbers, and E-mail Addresses

Sometime during each worship service there should be a registration procedure that does not single out visitors but elicits feedback from all persons in worship. This is an opportunity for all persons in the church community to communicate with the church's leadership and staff. There should be spiritually mature persons in each section of the sanctuary who see it as their ministry to greet and care for newcomers. Further there must be a systematic, comprehensive and accurate record-keeping system for the constituency. When persons have been visiting regularly, you should know their names, addresses, phone numbers, e-mail addresses, which Sunday school classes they have attended (if any), which Sundays they have attended, and which Sundays they have missed. You should even get important information about their family life and needs.

14. Preach Biblically and Evangelistically

Preaching should be well done and biblical. The topics most directly related to the way of salvation should get regular and repeated attention. The preacher should assume that some of the audience are non-Christians, and frequent invitations to commitment or recommitment are appropriate. The use of testimonies of how different persons have experienced God in their lives can serve to build up the faith and Christian experience of others. There are dangers here, and the use of testimonies has declined in some places because of abuses in the past. However, when they are used to build up the church, they can make an important difference.

15. Communicate Effectively in the Sermon

The sermon remains one of the most important ways in which evangelism is done. But communication is always culturally specific, and the preacher should use careful judgment about the ways in which preaching is most effective in his or her context. Because of the prevalence of television, effectiveness now suggests that the speaker not use any notes, nor read from a manuscript. For the same reason, video clips and drama may enhance communication of the gospel, but these are not ends in themselves. Because evangelism is based on love, there is no substitute for knowing one's people.

16. Respond Quickly and Appropriately to First-time Visitors

Evangelism concerns relationships, and when an overture is made there should be a proper response. Someone visiting the congregation comes for a variety of reasons, and one of the most important questions is, "Will I fit in here and will they welcome me?" To answer this question there should be a response made to first-time visitors within 36 hours—either by telephone or in person, depending on the culture. At some point—perhaps toward the end of the first week—there should be contact with a pastor, either by letter or by telephone call. The ideal model is to establish repeated, continuing contact with the same spiritually mature friend to help in the evangelistic and discipling processes.

17. Establish and Maintain Significant Small Groups for Seekers

While worship is the place in which the community gathers and God is praised in ways that both communicate who God is and how this community lives out its faith, there is an inescapable role for small-group conversation in the evangelism process. Establish regularly scheduled Alpha groups, or some other program to teach the basics of the faith. There should be multiple evangelistic groups, including Bible studies, Sunday school classes, disciple groups, twelve-step support groups, mission teams, and food pantry volunteer groups. Every small group for seekers should include all aspects of initiation into the Christian life. They should enable the seeker to connect with spiritually mature friends who nurture the person toward a deeper relationship with Christ and the church.

18. Give Appropriately Timed Invitations to Commitment

When the time is right, be sure to ask for a commitment with gentleness and reverence (1 Pet. 3:15-16). Communicate the community's expectation of what the Christian life is like, including all three steps with seven aspects of discipleship. Do not be guilty of false advertising. Stress the sacramental/liturgical aspects of baptism, confirmation, and joining the church.

19. Establish and Maintain a System of Discipleship for New Christians and New Members

Have high and clear expectations for membership in the Body of Christ. Have formation processes that regularly nurture those attitudes and behaviors with systems of accountability.

20. Establish and Maintain Small Groups for Growth in Discipleship and Service

Every believer should be involved in an intentional small group activity to continue discipleship growth. These will probably overlap with groups for seekers. Each group should understand its function in relation to the missional culture of the congregation. Each small group must play some role in the missional tasks of evangelism, nurture, and service. Ideally each small group has five functions: prayer, study, fellowship, accountability, and service.[9]

Evaluating Evangelistic Practice

The evaluation of evangelistic effectiveness is complex. It cannot focus simply on numbers, because there is always the possibility that successful evangelism sometimes means rejection of the message. If the culture is caught up with greed and prosperity, preaching the genuine gospel of Christ may not be attractive. To defend Jews in Nazi Germany was the proper Christian response, but the culture of that society was moving in a different direction under Hitler's leadership. Faithfulness to the gospel must always take precedence over church growth. We presume that one leads to the other, but there are times and places where faithfulness will generate unpopularity.

Thus, the proper way to measure the evangelistic success of a congregation is to ask if it is seeking to make disciples of Jesus Christ. The twenty components are one set of guidelines for looking at how congregations can effectively offer the gospel. While these practices have the intention of initiating persons into Christian discipleship, there is no guarantee that those being evangelized will respond positively.

The answers to six questions can summarize the overall approach to a congregation's effectiveness in this area.

Is this a missionary congregation?

How is the Holy Spirit's presence acknowledged?

How is the reign of God experienced and proclaimed?

How hospitable is the congregation?

How invitational is the congregation?

Does the congregation fully initiate new Christians?

In chapter 3 we saw that entering the Christian life involves seven aspects. It is not simply joining the church or being baptized or adopting a new, morally correct lifestyle. Rather, becoming Christian involves all seven aspects—baptism, cognitive commitments, spiritual disciplines, conversion, morality, spiritual gifts, and faith-sharing. To enter into the Christian life without one of them renders one's commitment incomplete.

An evangelistically successful congregation will have systems in place to help persons in each of these areas. It will communicate to those seeking Christian identity that it expects at least a beginning in all seven aspects. An evangelistically effective congregation will use a variety of ways aimed at initiating non-Christians into Christian discipleship in response to the reign of God. It will embody the way of life taught by Jesus and lovingly invite all others to participate so that they may also find the eternal life that Christ promised.

Notes

Foreword

1. Jones 2000, 7-8.

Introduction

1. John Deschner first helped me to see how fundamental this question is for the study of evangelism.
2. Quoted in Barrett, 49.
3. Barrett, 54.
4. Klaiber, 19.
5. Ibid., 20.
6. Abraham 1989, 95.

1. God's Evangelistic Love

1. Barrett, 77.
2. Barrett concludes that in most current English usage "'evangelism' is usually used only in reference to human evangelistic activity. 'Evangelization' has a broader meaning and refers to the whole range of evangelizing activity, both human and divine, as well as the overall situation and status produced by such activities," (78). In recent literature, "evangelization" has been preferred by writers associated with the World Council of Churches and the Roman Catholic Church while "evangelism" is the preferred term among evangelical Protestants in the United States. Barrett's survey shows that persons like John R. Mott could repeat the watchword of the Student Volunteer Movement—"the evangelization

of the world in this generation"—and mean by it something quite different from those using the term today.

3. Friedrich, 718. However Barth, 872, suggests that *euangelizesthai* is distinguished from *kerussein* because with the former the content is emphasized.

4. Friedrich, 720.

5. Armstrong, 37.

6. Ibid., 53.

7. Ibid., 63.

8. Nel, 33.

9. Ibid., 32.

10. Johnson, 21-22.

11. Ibid., 23.

12. Poe, 9.

13. Arias, 3.

14. Ibid., 12.

15. Ibid., xiii.

16. Ibid., xvi.

17. Ibid., 27.

18. Cullmann, 84.

19. Arias, 89.

20. Ibid., 92.

21. Ibid., 105-6.

22. Ibid., 111-12.

23. Abraham 1989, 17.

24. Ibid., 37.

25. Ibid., 38.

26. Kelsey, 106.

27. I have discussed John Wesley's understanding of the wholeness of Scripture in Jones 1995, 43-53, and used this as an organizing idea to account for the center of the doctrine of the United Methodist Church in Jones 2002, 59-64, 77-78.

28. Klaiber, 29.

29. Ibid., 75.

30. Ibid., 77.

31. Wesley *Notes,* 1 John 4:8.

32. For one understanding of this teaching, see Moltmann, 58-59.

33. E.g., Exod. 20:3, Deut. 31:20, and Jer. 1:16.

34. E.g., Deut. 24:17-21, Jer. 7:6, and Jer. 22:3.

35. E.g., Exod. 22:22, Deut. 10:18, and Deut. 27:19.

36. Rom. 1:18–2:11. See Rom. 3:23, "For all have sinned and fall short of the glory of God."

37. Brueggemann 1994, 839, 849.

38. For other examples, see Amos 2:6-8 and Zech. 7:10.

39. For the phrase "gracious and merciful, slow to anger and abounding in steadfast love," see Ps. 103:8.

40. Klaiber, 56.

41. Whether or not Paul wrote Colossians, its author stands in the Pauline tradition of early Christianity.

42. Bosch 1991, 30.

43. Ibid., 1.

44. John 14:16, NRSV, NIV, and KJV respectively.

2. Humanity's Evangelistic Love of God and Neighbor

1. Metzger and Murphy, in a footnote to *The New Oxford Annotated Bible* at John 7:53–8:11 say, "This account, omitted in many ancient manuscripts, appears to be an authentic incident in Jesus' ministry, though not belonging originally to John's Gospel." See Brown, 1:335-36 for a similar view.

2. O'Day, 296.

3. NRSV has the first reading in the text and the second in a footnote.

4. Brueggemann 1993, 38.

5. Bultmann, 208.

6. Article VII "Of the Old Testament" of the Church of England's Thirty-nine Articles and Article VI "Of the Old Testament" of the Articles of the Religion of the United Methodist Church (*Book of Discipline*, 61) both distinguish between the civil, moral, and ceremonial parts of the Old Testament Law. For a comment on the history of the distinction see Jones 1995, 238. There I cite sources suggesting it is at least as old as Irenaeus and Justin Martyr.

7. See parallels at Matt. 22:34-40 and Luke 10:25-28.

8. Boring, 424.

9. Ibid.

10. Ibid. See also Perkins, 678.

11. This becomes apparent at Luke 18:24 where the same question about eternal life is asked. Here, Jesus repeats the commandments from the Decalogue and then tells the ruler to give his money to the poor. When the ruler was saddened by this, Jesus said, "How hard it is for those who have wealth to enter the kingdom of God." Inheriting eternal life and entering the kingdom are treated as equivalent by Luke.

12. See John 14:18-31. The timing of the coming of the Spirit, whether it was given by the risen Christ (John 20:22) or at Pentecost (Acts 1) or whether both are true is immaterial to this point.

13. Bosch 1991, 10.

14. Cardoza-Orlandi, 45.

15. Ibid., 46-47.

16. Cardoza-Orlandi, 42.

17. Personal report, confirmed by communication with William J. Abraham.

18. I am indebted to Kenneth Cracknell for this insight.

19. Bosch, 15-16.

20. Ibid.

21. Keck, 25.

22. Augustine, 31.

23. Thompson, 6.

24. See Putnam for an extended analysis of the crisis in community in the United States at the end of the twentieth century. The ways in which evangelism builds community are an important aspect of the church's ministry.

25. Bosch 1991, 10.

26. Ibid., 411-12.

27. Robert, 4.

28. Ibid.

29. Pope-Levison, 165.

30. See also Rom. 12:13.

31. Klaiber, 198-99.

32. Ibid., 199.

33. *Book of Discipline of the United Methodist Church 2000*, 87-88.

3. *The Logic of Discipleship*

1. Abraham 1989, 93-94. Abraham calls the sharing of testimony "witness," using the word in a more restrictive sense than I have used it here.

2. Ibid., 94.

3. Ibid.

4. Ibid., 95.

5. Ibid., 96.

6. Ibid.

7. He argues that this should not be confused with liturgical rites of initiation. I am using "initiation" in the same sense and agree with his distinction.

8. Abraham 1989, 98-99.

9. Ibid., 101.

10. Ibid., 103. See his discussion of each of these aspects on pp. 117-63.

11. Ibid., 103.

12. Ibid., 104.

13. Abraham 1999, 158.

14. Ibid., 159.

15. Ibid.

16. Ibid.

17. Ibid., 160.

18. Ibid., 160-61.

19. Abraham 1989, 94.

20. Abraham 1999, 159.

21. One could avoid this conceptual difficulty by defining "church" as an invisible community of persons. Following Rahner's definition of an anonymous Christian (Rahner, 131) one could argue that all such persons collectively form the church. However, such a definition violates the general tenor of both Abraham's and my proposals.

22. Jones 2002, 60.

23. Logan 1994, 20.

24. Wesley *Works*, 2:156-57.

25. For a helpful way of understanding deeds of mercy as concrete expressions of prevenient grace, see Gunter 1999.

26. Hütter's understanding of theology as a church practice grounded in faith is an important reversal from much of contemporary theology. He says, "Not only does God's action 'determine' human beings qualitatively (as regards accidents), it also creates them as both creature and as new creation. This human pathos (and that of the theologian) corresponds to God's own poiesis, the poiesis of the Holy Spirit to which all theology is subjected and which is presented to theology in a quite specific way," 31.

27. Alpha is a program intended to help non-Christians explore Christian faith. Started by the Church of England parish of Holy Trinity, Brompton Road in London, it is now being used widely by many denominations. For information see www.alphana.org. For a critical evaluation, see Hunt.

28. See Rom. 8:14-17, 2 Cor. 5:17, 1 Pet. 2:10, and John 3:21.

29. Wesley *Works*, 2:157.

30. Ibid., 9:227.

31. World Council of Churches 1982, §B2.

32. In the case of young children or those with mental disabilities, exceptions are made because God knows their hearts better than we do.

33. Abraham 1989, 143.

34. Ibid., 147.

35. I have explained my understanding of the way in which theological reflection contributes to doctrinal development and reinvigoration in Jones 2002, 292-96.

36. Keck, 30-31.

37. Dawn, 80. The reference is to Temple, 68.

38. Dawn, 80-81.

39. Wesley *Works*, 3:428-30.

40. Ibid., 1:381.

41. Thompson, 33.

42. Ibid., 32.

43. See also Matt 9:15 concerning what the disciples will do after Jesus is gone.

44. Thompson, 71.

45. Abraham 1989, 120-21.

46. Miguez-Bonino, 329-30.

47. Ibid., 332.

48. Wesley *Works*, 9:70.

49. Albin, 278.

50. Matthaei 2001, 197.

51. Matthaei 2000, 166-73.

52. Bosch 1991, 117.

53. González and Gunsalus, 50.

54. Fowl and Jones, 14.

55. Ibid., 15.

56. Ibid., 20.

57. Bosch 1991, 8-9. The second quotation makes reference to J. C. Hoekendijk, *Kirche und Volk in der deutschen Missionswissenschaft*, Munich: Chr. Kaiser Verlag, 1967, 338.

58. Wesley *Works*, 9:70-73. For each of the rules, specific applications were given.

59. Dabney.

60. Thompson, 122.

61. See Michael Green 1990, 429-58 for a helpful discussion of what he calls "Discovery Groups."

4. Evangelism as Initiation into Christian Discipleship

1. Barrett, 23.

2. Ibid.

3. Ibid., 27.

4. Bosch 1991, 409-10. Bosch's suggestion here is a very seminal one that deserves serious research. I suspect that one of the ways in which the Evangelical Revival in England (and related movements elsewhere) led to the development of evangelism was the distinction that Wesley and others made to say that the average English person was not a real Christian. By distinguishing between nominal Christianity and real Christianity, Wesley and others were moving into modernity where Christian identity was not conveyed either sacramentally or by belonging to a Christian group (nation, tribe, or political unit) but by a personal act of faith that was an individual choice. Clearly these thinkers were building on the inheritance of Puritans and Pietists, but the stakes were being raised and the threshold of what counted as being Christian was going higher. As modernity advanced and the individual's relation to the larger culture changed, Protestant Christianity adapted its understandings of who was *really* a Christian. At the same time, as the United States expanded to the West, the establishment of certain Christian churches in the colonies gave way to the new evangelism as a form of nation building.

5. Bosch 1984, 166-68.

6. Bosch 1991, 411-20.

7. Mott, 4.

8. Barrett reprints shortened versions of 79 of these replies, pp. 42-46.

9. Mott, 4-5.

10. Salter does not identify the author of this statement, but it is John M. Springer, Bishop of the Methodist Episcopal Church in Africa. See Mott, 62.

11. Salter, 22.

12. Ibid., from Packer, 41.

13. Salter, 23.

14. Finney, xi.

15. John 3:8, "The wind blows where it chooses, and you hear the sound of it, but you do not know where it comes from or where it goes. So it is with everyone who is born of the Spirit."

16. McGavran, 23.

17. Ibid., 6.

18. Ibid., 87.
19. Hunter 1996, 28.
20. Ibid., 13.
21. Ibid.
22. Ibid., 25.
23. Ibid., 29, 32.
24. Ibid., 16.
25. Brueggemann, 45.
26. Hamilton, 97.
27. Ruffcorn, 16.
28. Ibid., 18.
29. Ibid., 20.
30. Klaiber, 26.
31. Abraham 1989, 95.
32. Ibid., 101.
33. Schaff, 3:592-95.
34. Van den Berg, 144-65.
35. Wesley *Works*, 7:704.
36. Niles, 96.

5. Evangelism as Necessarily Enculturated

1. I regard "enculturation" and "contextualization" as equivalent words and will use them interchangeably.
2. Robert, 5.
3. Bosch 1991, 28.
4. Ibid., 44. The final quotation is from Meyer, 206.
5. *United Methodist Hymnal*, 880.
6. Walls, 25.
7. Kulah, 154.
8. Oduyoye, 22.
9. See Putnam for a brilliant exposition of this phenomenon and its causes. His summation of causes is given at 277-83.
10. "For thou has made us for thyself and restless is our heart until it comes to rest in thee," Augustine, 31.
11. Hunter, 29.
12. Kenneson and Street, 16.
13. Ibid., 35.
14. Ibid., 72.
15. Ibid., 75-76.
16. Ibid., 101.
17. McGavran, x.
18. Ibid., 69.
19. Kenneson and Street, 93, 96.
20. Hunter, 59-60.
21. Kenneson and Street, 146.

22. Ruffcorn, 29-35.
23. Pedraja, 15.
24. Ibid., 71-72.
25. Saenz, 10-11.
26. Ibid., 11.

6. Evangelism and Ecclesiology

1. Wesley 1872, 14:321-22.
2. The word *teleios* and its cognates in the New Testament are sometimes translated as "mature" as in Eph. 4:13, Phil. 3:15, Col. 1:28, Col. 4:12, and James 1:4. In other places it is translated as "perfect," as in Matt. 5:48, Rom. 12:2, James 1:17, and James 1:25. In contemporary English, I regard "mature" as the better expression of what these texts have in mind for the goal of human spiritual growth because of the static connotations of the word "perfect." Nevertheless, taking Christ's commandment in Matt. 5:48 seriously is an important part of Christian discipleship.
3. See Phil. 3:15, Matt. 5:48, Phil. 2:5, 1 Thess. 4:3, and 1 Pet. 2:9.
4. Heb. 12:1, 1 Pet. 2:2, and Gal. 5:25.
5. See Wesley's sermons to Oxford University, "The Almost Christian," and "Scriptural Christianity," Wesley *Works*, 1:131-41 and 1:159-80.
6. Wesley *Works*, 2:196-98.
7. From Minutes of the Presbyterian Church (U.S.A.), 1995, Part I (Office of the General Assembly), 64.
8. *Book of Resolutions of the United Methodist Church*, 115.
9. Hare-Diggs.
10. Bosch 1991, 464.
11. See for example, the 1999 "Official Common Statement" on the Joint Declaration on the Doctrine of Justification by the Lutheran World Federation and the Catholic Church," www.lutheranworld.org/Special_Events/EN/gof99e.pdf.
12. Bosch 1991, 466.

7. Evangelism and Persons from Other Religions

1. For a helpful overview, see Pittman, Habito, and Muck, 42-53.
2. Smith, 111.
3. Pittman, Habito, and Muck, 54.
4. Mellor, in using these categories to evaluate John Wesley's views, calls them "blunt instruments," 111.
5. Pittman, Habito, and Muck, 55.
6. Ibid., 56.
7. Ibid., 58.
8. Ibid., 59.
9. Mellor, 120.
10. Abraham 1989, 226.
11. Abraham cites The Oxford English Dictionary, XI, 12.

12. Abraham 1989, 226.
13. Bosch 1991, 28, 30.
14. Mellor, 117.
15. Temple, 10.
16. Lindbeck, 59.
17. See Edward Said for a helpful discussion of these issues.
18. Niles, 96.
19. Bosch 1991, 420.
20. Charry, 170.
21. Ibid., 173.
22. Ibid., 176.
23. Ibid., 177.
24. Ibid., 178.
25. Ibid.
26. Ibid., 191-92.
27. Ibid., 174.
28. Marshall, 82.
29. Ibid., 94.
30. Ibid., 89. He cites Karl Barth saying that "though he remained a supersessionist, [he] was prompted by his reading of Paul to reject Christian missions to the Jews" (cf. *Church Dogmatics*, vol. IV, part 3, pp. 876-78).
31. Said, 12.
32. Kessler, 321.
33. World Council of Churches, §18, p. 10.
34. WCC, §19, p. 11.
35. Abraham 1989, 228.
36. Ibid., 228.
37. Personal report, confirmed with Cracknell.
38. Pittman, Habito, and Muck, 3-18.

Appendix

1. David Bosch, 375, attributes this to Temple, citing Stephen Neill, *The Church and Christian Union* (London: Oxford University Press, 1968), 76.
2. Senge, 18-19.
3. Ibid., 68.
4. Warren, 95-101.
5. Ibid., 111.
6. Rhodes, 20-21.
7. Michael Green has guidelines for this kind of witnessing, 489-526.
8. Boomershine, 88-90.
9. See Wills for a discussion of Wesley Groups.

Selected Bibliography

Abraham, William J.
1989   *The Logic of Evangelism*. Grand Rapids, Mich.: Eerdmans.
1990   "Athens, Aldersgate, and SMU: Reflections on the Place of
        Evangelism in the Theological Encyclopedia." *Journal of the Academy
        for Evangelism in Theological Education*. 5:65-75.
1994   "A Theology of Evangelism: The Heart of the Matter." *Interpretation*.
        48:117-30.
1999   "On Making Disciples of the Lord Jesus Christ," pp. 150-66 in Carl E.
        Braaten and Robert W. Jenson, eds. *Marks of the Body of Christ*. Grand
        Rapids, Mich. and Cambridge, UK: Eerdmans.
2001   "I Believe in One Holy, Catholic, and Apostolic Church," pp. 177-87
        in Christopher Seitz, ed. *Nicene Christianity: The Future for a New
        Ecumenism*. Grand Rapids, Mich.: Brazos.
Albin, Tom
1985   "An Empirical Study of Early Methodist Spirituality," pp. 275-90 in
        Wesleyan Theology Today: A Bicentennial Theological Consultation. Ed.
        Theodore Runyon. Nashville: Kingswood Books.
Alpha   http://www.alphana.org.
Amaladoss, Michael
1996   "Dialogue and Mission: Conflict or Convergence?" pp. 297-303 in
        Pittman, Habito, and Muck. Condensed from *International Review of
        Mission*, July 1986, 222-41.
Anscombe, G. E. M.
1974   *Intention*. 2nd ed. Ithaca, N.Y.: Cornell Univ. Press.
Arias, Mortimer
1984   *Announcing the Reign of God: Evangelization and the Subversive Memory
        of Jesus*. Philadelphia: Fortress.

Armstrong, Richard Stoll
    1979   *Service Evangelism*. Philadelphia: Westminster.
Augustine
    1955   *Augustine: Confessions and Enchiridion*. Trans. and ed. Albert C. Outler. Library of Christian Classics. Philadelphia: Westminster.
Bakke, Ray and Jim Hart
    1987   *The Urban Christian: Effective Ministry in Today's Urban World*. Downer's Grove, Ill.: Intervarsity.
Barrett, David B.
    1987   *Evangelize!: A Historical Survey of the Concept*. AD 2000 Series. Birmingham, Ala.: New Hope.
Barth, Karl
    1962   *The Doctrine of Reconciliation. Church Dogmatics*, Volume IV, 3, 2. Trans. G. W. Bromiley. Edinburgh: T. & T. Clark.
Berg, Johannes van den
    1956   *Constrained by Jesus' Love: An Inquiry into the Motives of the Missionary Awakening in Great Britain in the Period Between 1698 and 1815*. Kampen: J. H. Kok.
Book of Discipline of the United Methodist Church, 2000
    2000   Ed. Harriett Jane Olson, et al. Nashville: United Methodist Publishing House.
Book of Resolutions of the United Methodist Church, 2000
    2000   Nashville: United Methodist Publishing House.
Boomershine, Thomas E.
    1999   "Does United Methodism Have a Future in an Electronic Culture?" in *Questions for the Twenty-first Century Church*, ed. Russell E. Richey et al. Nashville: Abingdon, 79-90.
Boring, M. Eugene
    1995   "The Gospel of Matthew: Introduction, Commentary and Reflections." *The New Interpreter's Bible*. 8:87-505. Nashville: Abingdon.
Bosch, David J.
    1984   "Mission and Evangelism: Clarifying the Concepts," *Zeitschrift für Missionswissenschaft und Religionswissenschaft* 68 (July 1984):161-91.
    1991   *Transforming Mission: Paradigm Shifts in Theology of Mission*. American Society of Missiology Series, No. 16. Maryknoll, N.Y.: Orbis Books.
Brown, Ray
    1966–70 *The Gospel According to John*. 2 vols. Anchor Bible. Garden City, N.Y.: Doubleday.
Brueggemann, Walter
    1993   *Biblical Perspectives on Evangelism: Living in a Three-Storied Universe*. Nashville: Abingdon.
    1994   "The Book of Exodus: Introduction, Commentary and Reflections." pp. 1:675-981 in *The New Interpreters Bible*. Nashville: Abingdon.
Bultmann, Rudolf
    1968   "πιστεύω" in Gerhard Kittle, ed., *Theologisches Wörterbuch zum Neuen*

Testament, trans. Geoffrey W. Bromiley, *Theological Dictionary of the New Testament*. Grand Rapids, Mich.: Eerdmans. Vol. 6:174-82, 197-228.

Callahan, Kennon L.
1983   *Twelve Keys to an Effective Church: Strategic Planning for Mission.* San Francisco: Harper & Row.

Cardoza-Orlandi, Carlos F.
2002   *Mission: An Essential Guide.* Nashville: Abingdon.

Charry, Ellen T.
1993   "Two Millennia Later: Evangelizing Jews?" pp. 169-93 in Radner and Sumner.

Collins, Kenneth and John H. Tyson
2001   *Conversion in the Wesleyan Tradition.* Nashville: Abingdon.

Costas, Orlando E.
1989   *Liberating News: A Theology of Contextual Evangelization.* Grand Rapids, Mich.: Eerdmans.

Cullmann, Oscar
1962   *Christ and Time: The Primitive Christian Conception of Time and History.* Rev. ed. Trans. Floyd V. Filson. London: SCM.

Cracknell, Kenneth
1992   "Protestant Evangelism or Catholic Evanglization?: A Study in Methodist Approaches." [n.p.]: Methodist Sacramental Fellowship.

Dabney, D. Lyle
2001   "Unfinished Business: John Wesley and Friedrich Schleiermacher on the Doctrine of the Holy Spirit." www.wesleyanstudies.org, posted 2 March, 2001.

Dawn, Marva J.
1995   *Reaching Out Without Dumbing Down: A Theology of Worship for the Turn-of-the-Century Culture.* Grand Rapids, Mich.: Eerdmans.

Deck, Allan Figueroa
1989   *The Second Wave: Hispanic Ministry and the Evangelization of Cultures.* New York: Paulist Press.

Donovan, Vincent J.
1984   *Christianity Rediscovered.* 2nd edn. Maryknoll, N.Y.: Orbis Books.

Finney, Charles G.
1960   *Lectures on Revivals of Religion.* Ed. William G. McLoughlin. John Harvard Library. Cambridge, Mass.: Harvard University Press.

Forward, Martin, Stephen Plant, and Susan White, eds.
2000   *A Great Commission: Christian Hope and Religious Diversity: Papers in Honour of Kenneth Cracknell on his 65th Birthday.* Oxford: Peter Lang.

Fowl, Stephen E. and L. Gregory Jones
1991   *Reading in Communion: Scripture and Ethics in Christian Life.* Grand Rapids, Mich.: Eerdmans.

Friedrich, Gerhard
1964   "εὐαγγελίζομαι" in Gerhard Kittle, ed., *Theologisches Wörterbuch zum*

Neuen Testament, trans. Geoffrey W. Bromiley, *Theological Dictionary of the New Testament*. Grand Rapids, Mich.: Eerdmans. Vol. 2:707-17.

González, Justo L. and Catherine Gunsalus

    1980   *Liberation Preaching: The Pulpit and the Oppressed*. Abingdon Preacher's Library. Nashville: Abingdon.

Green, Bryan

    1951   "Evangelistic Preaching," in *The Practice of Evangelism*. London: Hodder and Stoughton.

Green, Michael

    1970   *Evangelism in the Early Church*. Grand Rapids, Mich.: Eerdmans.

    1990   *Evangelism Through the Local Church*. London: Hodder and Stoughton.

Guder, Darrell. L., et al.

    1998   *Missional Church: A Vision for the Sending of the Church in North America*. Grand Rapids, Mich. and Cambridge, UK: Eerdmans.

Gunter, W. Stephen

    1997   "Evangelism as the Heart of Mission: A Response to Dana L. Robert." in Dana L. Robert. *Evangelism as the Heart of Mission*. Mission Evangelism Series, Number 1. New York: General Board of Global Ministries, The United Methodist Church.

    1999   "Thinking Theologically About Evangelism." *Quarterly Review* 19:1 (Spring): 35-52.

Hamilton, Adam

    2002   *Leading Beyond the Walls: Developing Congregations with a Heart for the Unchurched*. Nashville: Abingdon.

Hare-Diggs, E. Brian and Jennifer L. Hare-Diggs

    2000   "Sacramental Faithfulness: Guidelines for Receiving People from the Church of Jesus Christ of Latter-Day Saints." General Board of Discipleship of the United Methodist Church. http://www.gbod.org/worship/articles/sacramental/default.htm.

Hunt, Stephen

    2001   *Anyone for Alpha?: Evangelism in a Post-Christian Society*. London: Dartman, Longman and Todd.

Hunter, George G., III

    1987   *To Spread the Power: Church Growth in the Wesleyan Spirit*. Nashville: Abingdon.

    1992   *How to Reach Secular People*. Nashville: Abingdon.

    1996   *Church for the Unchurched*. Nashville: Abingdon.

Hütter, Reinhard

    2000   *Suffering Divine Things: Theology as Church Practice*. Trans. Doug Stott. Grand Rapids, Mich.: Eerdmans.

Johnson, Ben Campbell

    1987   *Rethinking Evangelism: A Theological Approach*. Philadelphia: Westminster.

Jones, Scott

    1982   *Gathered Into One: The World Methodist Conference Speaks*. Nashville: Discipleship Resources.

1995   *John Wesley's Conception and Use of Scripture*. Kingswood Books. Nashville: Abingdon.

2000   "The Evangelistic Love of God and Neighbor." *Journal of the Academy for Evangelism in Theological Education* 15 (1999–2000): 6-17. Also at http://evangelism.smu.edu

2002   *United Methodist Doctrine: The Extreme Center*. Nashville: Abingdon.

Keck, Leander E.

1993   *The Church Confident*. Nashville: Abingdon.

Kelsey, David H.

1975   *The Uses of Scripture in Recent Theology*. Philadelphia: Fortress.

Kenneson, Philip D. and James L. Street

1997   *Selling Out the Church: The Dangers of Church Marketing*. Nashville: Abingdon.

Kessler, Edward D.

2000   "A Theology of Jewish-Christian Dialogue," pp. 319-32 in Forward, Plant, and White, eds.

Klaiber, Walter

1997   *Call and Response: Biblical Foundations of a Theology of Evangelism*. Trans. Howard Perry-Trauthig and James A. Dwyer. Nashville: Abingdon.

Kulah, Arthur F.

1996   "The Global Gospel: A Response from an African Perspective," pp. 153-58 in Logan, 1996.

Lindbeck, George A.

1984   *The Nature of Doctrine: Religion and Theology in a Postliberal Age*. Philadelphia: Westminster.

Logan, James C., ed.

1994   *Theology and Evangelism in the Wesleyan Heritage*. Kingswood Books. Nashville: Abingdon.

1996   *Christ for the World: United Methodist Bishops Speak on Evangelism*. Kingswood Books. Nashville: Abingdon.

Marsden, George M.

1980   *Fundamentalism and American Culture: The Shaping of Twentieth-Century Evangelicalism, 1870–1925*. Oxford: Oxford University Press.

Marshall, Bruce D.

1997   "Christ and the Cultures: The Jewish People and Christian Theology," pp. 81-100 in Colin E. Gunton, ed. *The Cambridge Companion to Christian Doctrine*. Cambridge, UK: Cambridge University Press.

Mathison, John, ed.

1992   *Tried and True: Eleven Principles of Church Growth from Frazer Memorial United Methodist Church*. Nashville: Discipleship Resources.

Matthaei, Sondra Higgins

2000   *Making Disciples: Faith Formation in the Wesleyan Tradition*. Nashville: Abingdon.

2001   "Conversion: Possibility and Expectation," pp. 195-210 in Collins and Tyson.

McGavran, Donald A.
1990   *Understanding Church Growth.* Revised and edited by C. Peter Wagner. 3rd ed. Grand Rapids, Mich.: Eerdmans.

Mellor, G. Howard
1994   "Evangelism and Religious Pluralism in the Wesleyan Heritage," pp. 109-26 in James C. Logan, ed. *Theology and Evangelism in the Wesleyan Heritage.* Kingswood Books. Nashville: Abingdon.

Metzger, Bruce M. and Roland E. Murphy, eds.
1991   *The New Oxford Annotated Bible Containing the Old and New Testaments, New Revised Standard Version.* New York: Oxford University Press.

Meyer, Ben F.
1986   *The Early Christians: Their World Mission and Self-Discovery.* Wilmington, Del.: Michael Glazier.

Miguez-Bonino, José
1983   "Conversion, New Creature and Commitment." *International Review of Mission.* 72: 324-32.

Moltmann, Jürgen
1981   *The Trinity and the Kingdom: The Doctrine of God.* Trans. Margaret Kohl. San Francisco: Harper and Row.

Mott, John R., ed.
1938   *Evangelism for the World Today, As Interpreted by Christian Leaders Throughout the World.* For the International Missionary Council. New York and London: Harper and Brothers.

Nel, Malan
1998   "Service Evangelism: The Theology and Methodology of a Lifestyle." *Journal of the Academy for Evangelism in Theological Education* 13 (1997–98): 33.

Newbigin, Lesslie
1989   *The Gospel in a Pluralist Society.* Grand Rapids, Mich.: Eerdmans.

Niles, Daniel Thambyrajah
1951   *That They May Have Life.* New York: Harper and Brothers.

O'Day, Gail R.
1992   "John." In *The Women's Bible Commentary.* Ed. Carol A. Newsom and Sharon H. Ringe. Louisville, Ky.: Westminster/John Knox.

Oduyoye, Mercy Amba
1997   "Evangelism as the Heart of Mission: A Response to Dana Robert," pp. 21-26 in Dana L. Robert, *Evangelism as the Heart of Mission.* Mission Evangelism Series, Number 1. New York: General Board of Global Ministries, The United Methodist Church.

Packer, J. I.
1967   *Evangelism and the Sovereignty of God.* Chicago: Intervarsity.

Pedraja, Luis G.
1999   *Jesus Is My Uncle: Christology from a Hispanic Perspective.* Nashville: Abingdon.

Perkins, Pheme
    1995   "The Gospel of Mark: Introduction, Commentary and Reflections,"
            pp. 8:507-733 in *The New Interpreter's Bible*. Nashville: Abingdon.
Pittman, Don A., Ruben L. F. Habito, and Terry C. Muck, eds.
    1996   *Ministry and Theology in Global Perspective: Contemporary Challenges for*
            the Church. Grand Rapids, Mich. and Cambridge, UK: Eerdmans.
Poe, Harry L.
    1996   *The Gospel and Its Meaning: A Theology for Evangelism and Church*
            Growth. Grand Rapids, Mich.: Zondervan.
Pope-Levison, Priscilla
    1991   *Evangelization from a Liberation Perspective*. New York: Peter Lang.
Putnam, Robert D.
    2000   *Bowling Alone: The Collapse and Revival of American Community*. New
            York: Simon and Schuster.
Radner, Ephraim and George R. Sumner, eds.
    1993   *Reclaiming Faith: Essays on Orthodoxy in the Episcopal Church and the*
            Baltimore Declaration. Grand Rapids, Mich.: Eerdmans.
Rahner, Karl
    1966   *Theological Investigations*. Vol. V. *Later Writings*. Trans Karl-H. Kruger.
            Baltimore: Helicon and London: Darton, Longman, and Todd.
Rhodes, Stephen A.
    1998   *Where the Nations Meet: The Church in a Multicultural World*. Downers
            Grove, Ill.: Intervarsity.
Robert, Dana L.
    1997   *Evangelism as the Heart of Mission*. Mission Evangelism Series,
            Number 1. New York: General Board of Global Ministries of The
            United Methodist Church.
Ruffcorn, Kevin E.
    1994   *Rural Evangelism: Catching the Vision*. Minneapolis: Augsburg.
Runyon, Ted
    1998   *The New Creation: John Wesley's Theology Today*. Nashville: Abingdon.
Saenz, Ruben
    2002   "A Complex Calling: Evangelism with the Hispanic Community."
            Circuit Rider (Nov/Dec): 9-11.
Salter, Darius
    1996   *American Evangelism: Its Theology and Practice*. Grand Rapids, Mich.:
            Baker.
Said, Edward W.
    1978   *Orientalism*. New York: Pantheon Books.
Schaff, Philip
    1998   *Creeds of Christendom with a History and Critical Notes*. 3 vols. 6th edn.
            Rev. David S. Schaff. Grand Rapids, Mich.: Baker Books.
Schmidt, Jean Miller
    1991   *Souls Or The Social Order: The Two-Party System in American*
            Protestantism. Brooklyn, N.Y.: Carlson.

Senge, Peter M.
:   1990   *The Fifth Discipline: The Art and Practice of the Learning Organization.* New York: Doubleday.
Sider, Ronald
:   1977   *Evangelism, Salvation and Social Justice.* Bramcote, UK: Grove.
Smith, Timothy L.
:   1957   *Revivalism and Social Reform in Mid-nineteenth-century America.* New York: Abingdon.
Smith, Wilfred Cantwell
:   1965   *The Faith of Other Men.* New York: New American Library.
Stewart, Carlyle Fielding, III
:   1994   *African-American Church Growth: 12 Principles of Prophetic Ministry.* Nashville: Abingdon.
Temple, William
:   1949   *Readings in St. John's Gospel.* London: Macmillan.
Thompson, Marjorie J.
:   1995   *Soul Feast: An Invitation to the Christian Spiritual Life.* Louisville, Ky.: Westminster John Knox.
Tillich, Paul
:   1963   *Systematic Theology, Volume III: Life and the Spirit, History and the Kingdom of God.* Chicago: University of Chicago.
The United Methodist Hymnal: Book of United Methodist Worship
:   1989   Nashville: The United Methodist Publishing House.
Trueblood, Elton
:   1972   *The Validity of the Christian Mission.* New York: Harper & Row.
Van Gelder, Craig
:   2000   *The Essence of the Church: A Community Created by the Spirit.* Grand Rapids, Mich.: Baker Books.
Verkuyl, Johannes
:   1978   *Contemporary Missiology: An Introduction.* Translated and edited by Dale Cooper. Grand Rapids, Mich.: Eerdmans.
Walls, Andrew F.
:   1990   "The Translation Principle in Christian History," pp. 24-39 in P. C. Stine, ed. *Bible Translation and the Spread of the Church: The Last 200 Years.* Leiden and New York: Brill.
Warren, Richard
:   1995   *The Purpose Driven Church: Growth Without Compromising Your Message and Mission.* Grand Rapids, Mich.: Zondervan.
Wesley, John
:   1755   *Explanatory* Notes Upon the New Testament. London: William Bowyer, 1755. Various reprints, including http://wesley.nnu.edu. Referred to as Wesley, *Notes.*
:   1872   *The Works of John Wesley.* [Ed. Thomas Jackson]. 14 vols. London: Wesleyan Conference Office, 1872. Reprint. Grand Rapids, Mich.: Zondervan, 1958. Referred to as Wesley, *Works* (J).

1984–   *The Works of John Wesley.* Ed. Frank Baker and Richard P. Heitzenrater. Bicentennial Edition. Nashville: Abingdon. Referred to as Wesley, *Works.*

Wilke, Richard Byrd and Julia Kitchens
1993   *Disciple: Becoming Disciples Through Bible Study.* Second edn. Nashville: Abingdon.

Wills, Dick
1999   *Waking to God's Dream: Spiritual Leadership and Church Renewal.* Nashville: Abingdon.

World Council of Churches
1979   *Guidelines on Dialogue with People of Living Faiths.* Geneva: World Council of Churches. Also at http://www.wcc-coe.org/wcc/what/interreligious/ glines-e.html.

1982   *Baptism, Eucharist and Ministry.* Faith and Order Paper 111. Geneva: World Council of Churches. Also at http://www.wcc-coe.org/wcc/what/faith/bem1.html.

Index